The Method of Metaphor

T0345334

The Method of Metaphor

Stanley Raffel

intellect Bristol, UK / Chicago, USA

First published in the UK in 2013 by
Intellect, The Mill, Parnall Road, Fishponds, Bristol, BS16 3JG, UK

First published in the USA in 2013 by
Intellect, The University of Chicago Press, 1427 E. 60th Street,
Chicago, IL 60637, USA

A catalogue record for this book is available from the
British Library.

Cover designer: Stephanie Sarlos
Copy-editor: Emma Rhys
Production manager: Bethan Ball
Typesetting: Contentra Technologies

Part of the *Culture, Disease, and Well-Being: The Grey Zone of Health
and Illness* series
Series editor: Alan Blum
Series ISSN: 2042-177X
Electronic ISSN: 2042-1788

Print ISBN: 978-1-78320-014-6
ePDF ISBN: 978-1-78320-155-6
ePub ISBN: 978-1-78320-154-9

Printed and bound by Hobbs, UK

Contents

Acknowledgments   vii

Introduction   1

Chapter 1:   Metaphor in Dante   11

Chapter 2:   Metaphor in Fairy Tales   27

Chapter 3:   Sontag's Critique of Metaphors   39

Chapter 4:   Abortion   55

Chapter 5:   Metaphors and the Issue of Incommensurability   67

Chapter 6:   Israel and Palestine   81

Chapter 7:   The Problem of Evil   89

Chapter 8:   Tragedy vs Comedy   101

Chapter 9:   Teaching   111

Chapter 10: Oriented Action   123

Chapter 11: Bad Metaphors   133

References   143

Acknowledgments

I am indebted to Alan Blum for his reading of previous drafts. He demonstrated an uncanny ability to see what was still needed. Though Peter McHugh died before I began, both his method and his substantive ideas have strongly influenced this book. A group consisting of Eric Laurier, Allyson Noble, and Gregor Schnuer have offered sympathetic and perceptive criticisms of all my work. I am grateful to Kieran Bonner for many stimulating conversations over the years. A meeting of the Culture of Cities project in Toronto, Canada provided valuable feedback on several chapters. As the book neared completion, Steve Bailey made useful suggestions that have improved it. Without the encouragement of my wife, Elaine Samuel, I am certain I would never have finished this work and doubt I would even have started it.

Introduction

In making judgments, the tool it is supposedly most appropriate to employ is the syllogism. Its nature and use were first formally described and defended by Aristotle. Imagine, as in the classic example, you wish to decide whether a particular man will die. It is not enough just to identify him as Socrates because that just begs the question of whether Socrates will die. Only when one can satisfy oneself of two things, the so-called major premise that all men die and the so-called minor premise that Socrates is a man, is one in a position to confidently assert Socrates' mortality. The power—the compelling nature—of the conclusion stems not only from the derivation being logical but, equally, from our certainty that both the major and minor premises are clear-cut facts. We would not feel nearly so certain if the premises were nothing more than opinions.

Valid syllogisms are much more convincing ways of judging than the mere expression of an opinion. However, can they help us judge anything important? Writing in the 1980s, Alasdair Macintyre (Macintyre 1985: 6–7) identified a series of controversies, about the best way to maintain peace, about abortion, and about equal opportunities. What he found is that in each case, *both* sides were convinced that their judgments were right, precisely because their conclusions followed logically from their premises.

On the one hand, pacifism seems logical because (major premise) war cannot be just if there is too much collateral damage and (minor premise) modern wars will inevitably cause large amounts of such damage. On the other hand, pacifism is illogical because (major premise) it is necessary to deter potential aggressors and (minor premise) the only way to do so is to make it clear you are prepared to fight them.

Concerning abortion, it is wrong because (major premise) murder is wrong and (minor premise) abortion is murder. On the other hand, it is right because (major premise) we have the right to do what we will with our bodies and (minor premise) the embryo is part of a woman's body.

Turning to equal opportunity, ban private schools because (major premise) there cannot be justice without equal opportunity for all and (minor premise) so long as there are private schools, there will never be equal opportunity. On the other hand, don't ban them because (major premise) persons' personal freedom is precious and (minor premise) such a ban would grossly infringe on freedom.

Either in the same form or with minor variations, such controversies are still with us. Furthermore, there are innumerable other controversies—issues we must judge—that can be expressed as apparently valid syllogisms and yet remain equally controversial. That this is so suggests that, even though a willingness to conform to the demands of logic surely does lead to more rational judgments than the unconstrained expression of personal opinions, with regard to important issues the syllogistic method is apparently much less effective at producing anything like a meeting of minds than we (and probably Aristotle) might have thought.

While Macintyre is disturbed by the fact that persons who seem to him equally logical can reach such wildly different conclusions, what he does not notice is that there is actually something wrong with all these syllogisms. While all the conclusions probably do follow from the premises, none of the premises really qualify as definite facts. For example, that abortion is murder hardly is as definite a fact as that Socrates is a man. Nor does even the idea that murder is necessarily wrong have quite the same certitude as (the fact) that we are all going to die. The pro-choice syllogism is equally flawed: can we really be certain either that an embryo is best seen as part of the mother's body or, even if we can be, are we sure that we are necessarily free to do with our bodies what we will?

Furthermore, the premises on which the other conclusions are based are, if anything, even less plausible as definite facts. For example, who is to say that arms build-ups really do deter (as distinct even from cause) aggression; that one can never have a just war with huge civilian casualties; or that the existence of private schools is either a key obstacle to equal opportunity or an essential component of freedom?

Syllogistically derived conclusions are only sound if the facts they are premised on are sound and it does seem that, for the typical judgments we would wish to make, the relevant facts are rarely if ever forthcoming. While we do begin to see that, at least for many issues that matter, syllogisms are not providing as sound a way of judging as has been hoped, if we are not to revert to the view that all there are are unwarranted opinions, it is worth considering whether there might be an alternative way to judge. Introducing the third volume of *The Life of the Mind*, a work she never got to make more than a start on, Hannah Arendt wrote:

> I shall show that my main assumption in singling out judgement as a distinct capacity of our minds has been that judgements are not arrived at by either deduction or induction; in short they have nothing in common with logical operations—as when we say: All men are mortal, Socrates is a man, hence Socrates is mortal. We shall be in search of the 'silent sense' which—when it was dealt with at all—has always, even in Kant, been thought of as 'taste' and therefore as belonging to the realm of aesthetics. (Arendt 1978: 215)[1]

This is, to say the least, suggestive. Arendt is critiquing the whole tradition founded by Aristotle. It may be possible to find an alternative way to manage judgments besides syllogisms and this alternative will have to do with, in particular, taste, and, in general, the realm of aesthetics. Arendt's own version of how aesthetic techniques rather than syllogisms can be used in making judgments employs the idea of an exemplar:

> One may encounter or think of some table that one judges to be the best possible table and take this as the example of how tables should be: the *exemplary table* […] This exemplar

is and remains a particular that in its very particularity reveals the generality that otherwise could not be defined. Courage is *like* Achilles. Etc. (Arendt 1982: 77, original emphasis)

Achilles appears here as an ideal in accordance with which we can be judged. But, in various ways, this mode of judgment seems problematic. In that most of us are surely unlikely to manage *his* feats, there is the strong chance that, if judged in this way, virtually *no one* is likely to be judged courageous. Also, this way of judging courage will not be able to give them their due if, as there certainly are, there are different sorts of courage than his.

Furthermore, even for any who *can* be likened to Achilles, given that Achilles was lacking in other essential qualities such as temperance, it remains to be seen whether such people could actually be judged to be good. Arendt can be seen to be trying to rectify this problem in that she attempts to supplement her exemplar of courage with exemplars of goodness: 'If we say of somebody that he is good, we have in the back of our minds the example of Saint Francis or Jesus of Nazareth' (Arendt 1982: 84).

But, of course, if we need to be like these two to be good, as with trying to be like Achilles to be courageous, few if any will make the grade. Furthermore, forms of goodness that are unlike those of Jesus or Francis are sure to be overlooked.

There is another form of comparison besides relating phenomena to ideals that is a very familiar feature of aesthetic discourse. It has the additional benefit of requiring, even more clearly than does finding exemplars, the faculty Arendt sees as needed, taste. Instead of seeking to decide whether or not someone is like Achilles or Jesus, whether, in other words, they manage to achieve an ideal, one can seek, in open-ended fashion, to judge what they are actually like. That is to say, one can try to depict the nature of any one or any thing by searching for the right metaphor for them or it.

Besides being first to offer a formal version of the syllogism, Aristotle also wrote extensively about aesthetics. It is surely significant that, essential to aesthetics according to Aristotle is not the exemplar but 'the right use of metaphor' (Aristotle 1958: l.1459a, 49). However, Aristotle per se cannot offer the alternative to the syllogism that Arendt intuits the need for because, as Jacques Derrida shows, he disparages the kind of reasoning that uses metaphors in comparison with the best philosophy, which he identifies with the use of syllogisms. Metaphor is 'not as serious as philosophy itself' (Derrida 1982: 238). One should 'prefer the discourse of full truth to metaphor' (238). For example, Aristotle reproaches Plato for being satisfied with 'poetic metaphors' (238).[2]

Derrida goes on to explain why, in Aristotle's conception, if all one can manage are metaphors, one falls short of the truth. Metaphors

can manifest properties, can relate properties from the essence of different things to each other, can make them known on the basis of their resemblance, but nonetheless without directly, fully, and properly stating essence itself, without bringing to light the truth of the thing itself. (Derrida 1982: 249)

If all we can depict is what a thing or person is like, we still are not able, it seems, to depict what that thing actually-really-*is*.

That this remains a plausible way to understand what is wrong with metaphors, and so a potentially fatal flaw in utilizing them to make judgments, can be seen in the analysis of metaphor offered by a contemporary theorist, John Searle. Considering the metaphor 'Sally is a block of ice' (Searle 1979: 82), Searle suggests, and surely we must agree, that it cannot be literally true. In attempting to describe what Aristotle would consider the truth—the actual being—of Sally that could replace the metaphor, Searle offers what he calls a paraphrase: 'Sally is an extremely unemotional and unresponsive person' (82). However, he then concedes that 'the paraphrase is somehow inadequate [...] Something is lost' (82). Already, then, even though it does seem that the metaphor depicts, as Aristotle would expect, only what she is like, not what she really is, it is proving difficult to move from the likeness to an exact depiction of the reality.

Searle himself believes that the reason for the difficulty is no great mystery. It is because an existing language, in this case English, does not happen to have an 'exact device for expressing literally' whatever 'Sally is a block of ice' is trying to say (Searle 1979: 114). Searle offers another example that he thinks demonstrates that it is merely the happenstance of there being no exact word for Sally's condition that makes us unable to move from the metaphor to the way she really is. If we say 'Sally is tall,' have we not described a reality without resorting to a metaphor and is not that possible simply because, in this case, the exact word for what we want to say *does* exist (79)?

However, in contrast to how Searle interprets his example, even though 'tall' might be the perfect word to describe what one wants to say about Sally, there is a problem in accepting that the term designates her reality rather than what she is like. As Searle himself points out, 'a woman can be correctly described as "tall" even though she is shorter than a giraffe' (Searle 1979: 80). But *how* can such a description be correct? Only if, on reflection, we realize that even when we think we are managing to depict what Sally really is, there is an implicit claim that there is something to which she is '*similar* with respect to the property specified by the term' (81, emphasis added). In this case, she does not have to be similar to a giraffe but, unless the statement is to be deemed incorrect, she does have to be *like* 'all tall women' (81).

It will begin to seem less odd that whenever we try to say what Sally is, we end up not being able to be more precise than depicting what she is like if we realize that any judgment, even a description, requires assigning some value to an object, action, or person and specific values can only be arrived at by making comparisons. That Sally is a tall woman, for example, is arrived at by seeing she is like some women, quite unlike some other women, and also perhaps unlike tall men (in which case that she is tall might be considered an understatement). Her identity is constituted by all she is similar to and different from. It is by the comparisons that we depict her, it not being possible just to say without comparisons, what she is in herself. Drawing on de Saussure, Derrida makes this point well:

The signified concept is never present in and of itself, in sufficient presence that would refer only to itself. Essentially and lawfully, every concept is inscribed in a chain or in a system within which it refers to other concepts, by means of the systematic play of differences. (Derrida 1982: 11)

What Derrida is noting here has become for him and like-minded others more than just a way of understanding how meaning is achieved in everyday life. It has strongly influenced conceptions of what theorizing can and should be. For example, in his own theorizing—deconstruction—Derrida seeks to develop the meaning of texts precisely by this process of interpreting differences and similarities in the play of signifiers. It is by sticking to this procedure that he can claim to be interpreting the possible meaning of a text without there needing to be what he claims there can never be, a signifier that can directly make present what is signified.[3]

In work that predates Derrida's intervention, there is also the psychoanalyst Jacques Lacan's way of working out the meaning of what could potentially seem nonsensical, namely subjects' unconscious utterances. He too uses the idea of the lack of full presence of the signified. As Lacan puts it: 'No signification can be sustained other than by reference to another signification' (Lacan 1977: 150).

Furthermore, as one of the tools that must be used if one is to be able to work out what the seemingly nonsensical array of signifiers might mean, he explicitly mentions being alert to metaphors: 'Psychoanalysis is akin to poetry in which the interplay of metaphors is a major means of encountering unspeakable truth' (Benvenuto and Kennedy 1986: 119).[4]

Third, there is the form of sociological theory developed by Alan Blum and Peter McHugh, which can be described as seeking to display how the social actor could move from a kind of unconsciousness when acting to the full consciousness they call acting self-reflectively. In their work, they depict the actor they inherit from previous social theory as not fully conscious of what s/he is doing because this actor was considered socially competent when s/he was merely unreflectively complying with social rules—conventions—expectations. They say that only if the actor has a theory of the worth of what is undertaken, thereby 'reauthorizing convention through the agency of his decision to undertake it or not' (Blum and McHugh 1984: 116) can s/he qualify as fully conscious.

Where we can first see an affinity between their method and Derrida's and Lacan's is in it again being the case that the signified is never fully present because what appears to the actor, i.e. the signifiers, in this sociologically informed version are just the conventions rather than what could authorize the decision as to whether to follow them. Furthermore, there is the perhaps even more important similarity to Derrida and Lacan that their version of how one manages to see an action as other than merely conventional, as fully consciously undertaken, is when one can theorize 'the *difference* that would be made between its being undertaken or not' (Blum and McHugh 1984: 120, emphasis added). Or, as they further elaborate this version of seeing meaning-significance, to see the meaning of anything one needs the clarity of making 'explicit […] what belongs to it vis-à-vis […] what is other to it' (146).

There is also an affinity between these forms of theorizing and Arendt's. In the part of her work that she did get to complete, while the need to identify meaning by seeing differences and similarities does not feature, she could be said to be one of those who paves the way for the approach these others have taken in that she bases her entire analysis of the activity she calls thinking on the idea that it is an activity that 'is not inspired by the quest for truth but for the quest for meaning' (Arendt 1978: 15). To abandon the search for truth is equivalent to appreciating that the signified is never fully present, never available per se. It can be said that such an approach is a necessary precursor to an interest in metaphoric reasoning as a way of theorizing in that while it seems right that (as the other theorists cited have argued and as we shall see in the chapters that follow) seeing what X is like can help one identity what the *meaning* of X might be, that is not the same as discovering some definitive *truth* about X.

An additional resonance of Arendt's analysis of thinking is that, like Blum and McHugh's version of theorizing but unlike both Derrida's and Lacan's, without ever denying that thinking is an activity that can be absent on occasion or even frequently in our everyday lives, at the same time it is no technical procedure restricted to either deconstructionists or psychoanalysts. Instead it is an activity that all or at least most of us could engage in and, furthermore one that we will say in an argument that borrows heavily from Arendt, we actually *should* engage in. (See especially Chapter 7.)

If it is the case that the only way to judge what X is is to work out what X is like and unlike, we are relieved of Aristotle's concern that, if all we can manage are metaphors, what a thing really is escapes us. Apt metaphors can be said to depict what things are by depicting what they can credibly be likened to.

Realizing this point can be liberating. One would think that to theorize what any phenomenon is, merely articulating what it is like (not to mention what it is unlike) would not get one very far. On the other hand, with this different understanding of how a thing's being is constituted, i.e. by what it is different from and what it is similar to, one feels stimulated to search out valid comparisons because it is only by managing to do so that any thing's being can be illuminated.[5]

While none of the following studies would be possible without this insight, a glaring problem facing our employment of metaphoric reasoning for theorizing must be faced. Whatever the defects of attempting to judge with syllogisms, at least it seems clear when such judgments are faulty, i.e. either when the premises are not facts or, even if they are, when the conclusion does not follow from them. In that no metaphor is exactly factually correct or even logical, while there are surely faulty metaphors, it is much more difficult to say how one would recognize them. Even in an introduction, a way to at least begin to think about this issue is called for.

If the identity of any thing is a matter of what differentiates it from other things, unless what it is is obvious from its appearance, appearances must be potentially deceptive. If appearances were not potentially deceptive, the mere fact that X looks different from other things would establish that it must have a separate identity.

That appearances can be misleading means that to identify anything, to differentiate it adequately, we will need to notice things that it does not appear similar to that it may actually be like. Roughly speaking, a good metaphor would be one that helps us to see, in the sense of appreciate, unapparent—unobvious—similarities. Bad ones would claim resemblances in things that not only appear different but also do not have similarities that make us feel the apparent differences between the things *are* misleading. The implication of our admission that this criterion is rough is that we hope and believe it will become clearer as we go along. As a start on achieving such clarity, Chapter 1 will explore the work of someone who is adept, even masterful, at noticing similarities in things that, without his help, we would be convinced are quite different.

Notes

1   See also Arendt 1978: 255–72 and Arendt 1982. In addition, see Beiner and Nedelsky 2001; Beiner 1983; and Norval 2010.

2   For a more recent defense of syllogisms that depends on a critique of aesthetics, see Rudolf Carnap (1959). Our defense of an aesthetic approach both here and especially in Chapter 3 aligns us with Martin Heidegger's point that, as Arendt put it: 'Carnap's own evaluation may be based on an underestimation of poetry' (Arendt 1978: 8).

3   Derrida's colleague, Paul de Man, suggests that, if meaning is created in this way, that explains why not even those who attempt to eschew metaphors can avoid using them in their actual theorizing. See de Man (1978) and our own examples of this phenomenon in Chapters 3 and 10.

4   See also Lacan 1977: 156–8.

5   Paul Ricoeur's book on metaphor represents perhaps the major modern attempt to deny that this sort of theorizing is sufficient. He writes: 'In saying that this is (like) that […] the assimilation does not reach the level of an identity of meaning. The "similar" is not the "same"' (Ricoeur 1978: 296). Derrida would reply that such a view does not attend to how meaning is actually produced, i.e. by establishing differences. Another way to question the cogency of Ricoeur's point is Martin Heidegger's analysis of the same as whatever belongs together rather than whatever is identical (see Heidegger 1969). I would ask the reader to decide, in considering the studies that follow, whether, contrary to what Ricoeur would expect, the being of various actions and things is sufficiently revealed when we work out compelling resemblances between them.

Chapter 1

Metaphor in Dante

Our first example of a writer who manages to judge phenomena utilizing metaphors will be Dante in the three books of his *Divine Comedy*.

Inferno

While Dante is certainly not the first or last writer to imagine what happens to sinners in Hell, it has to be said that the punishments he invents are somehow distinctive. For example, hypocrites wear cloaks that 'Outwardly they were gilded dazzling-bright, /But all within was lead, and, weighed thereby' (Dante 1979: [c.1314] Canto XXIII, ll.64–5, 215).

Extreme flatterers such as the courtesan who, when asked by her lover: 'To what degree, have I earned thanks, my love?' replied: 'O, to a very miracle,' have dung coming out of their mouths (Dante 1979: Canto XVIII, ll.133–5, 185). Persons noteworthy for violent tempers are 'tearing each other piecemeal with their teeth' (Canto VII, l.114, 113). Those fated to be submerged in a 'thick pitch', visible only as 'great bubbles black as ink' (Canto XXI, l.19, 201), turn out to have been notorious bribers who specialized in 'subsurface deals and secret money-grubbing' (Canto XXI, l.54, 202).

Attempting to depict what is special about Dante's treatment of these and other sinners, his translator, Dorothy Sayers, writes: 'The "punishment" for sin is simply the sin itself, experienced without illusion' (Dante 1979: 102, note by Sayers). In a similar vein, one of the best Dante interpreters, Charles Williams, writes: 'These punishments […] are, in some sense, the sin itself' (Williams 1943: 128).

While we will need to specify what Dante's method is for removing any 'illusion' and what 'some sense' could be referencing, both Sayers and Williams are right that Dante does have a way of getting us to experience the sin itself, i.e. its nature, its being. I suggest that he gets us to see what the sin is by managing to depict what it is *like*. It is, then, by finding an appropriate comparison—a good metaphor—that Dante manages to reveal the nature of these and other sins that place people in the Inferno. However, it is fair to say that not all the metaphors are quite as self-explanatory as the ones noted so far.

Sometimes it helps to know the specific cases of a sin that Dante has in mind. Thus, it begins to make more sense that Dante envisions suicides as trees with 'Discolored leaves and dark, no tender shoots, /But withered and gnarled and tough, no fruit' (Dante 1979: Canto XIII, ll.5–6, 149) once we learn that he is particularly thinking of 'a kind of "suicide wave" about Dante's time' that afflicted the young of Florence (155, note by Sayers).

We might guess that the fate of those so unable to stay separate from other people that they merge with them, taking the following form in Hell, are thieves: 'Ivy to oak never so rooted grew […] their tints began to mingle and to run/And neither seemed to be what it had been' (Dante 1979: Canto VIII, ll.58–63, 228).

However, it is still informative to learn that one of these thieves whose fate is for 'two faces to fuse themselves, to weld one countenance' (Dante 1979: Canto VIII, ll.71–2, 229) had as his modus operandi: 'to have got into people's houses, disguised as an old beggar' (301, note by Sayers). That is, his fate seems right because how he behaved is *like* not having a face of his own.

Sometimes it can be necessary to know how Dante understands the sin in order to appreciate how appropriate the metaphor is. Once we know that Dante saw heresy as 'an obduracy of the mind […] an intellectual obstinacy' (Williams 1943: 125, quoted in Dante 1979: 132, note by Sayers), it makes more sense that the fate of heretics is to be constantly forging an iron coffin for themselves. That is, confining themselves in this way is *like* what they are doing by being so obstinate.

Other times, local knowledge of the material out of which Dante composes his metaphors can improve our understanding. Once we know that

in Dante's church, the font in the Baptistery was surrounded by holes in which the officiating priests stood, so as not to be jostled by the crowds on days when a great number of bambinos were being baptized at once. (Dante 1979: 192, note by Sayers)

it becomes clearer why Dante imagines the fate of those who sold sacraments as being plunged headfirst into this type of hole. Selling such holy things is *like* turning one's priestly function upside down.

That Dante's way of understanding a sin is to find an appropriate metaphor for it also applies to what is said to be 'the greatest image in the whole Inferno' (Dante 1979: 275, note by Sayers). Traitors such as Judas and the devil himself are wedged in 'a lake so bound with ice, it did not look like water but like glass' (Canto XXXII, ll.23–4, 271). Sayers suggests how original this version of these sinners' fate is: 'The conception is, I think, Dante's own. Although the Apocalypse of Paul mentions a number of cold torments, these are indiscriminately mingled with the torments by fire and their placing has no structural significance' (275, note by Sayers).

Clearly, Dante's idea is that this is the fate of traitors because to be a traitor is *like* being ice cold, i.e. to not be able to be receptive even to the warmth that would inevitably be emanating from those closest to us.

As can be anticipated if the argument in the Introduction is sound, syllogisms would be of little use in judging these phenomena. For example, a minor premise that one could perhaps adopt in trying to demonstrate that extreme flattery or hypocrisy is wrong might be that these behaviors amount to lies. But this is debatable and, even if it could be established, it of course remains unclear that to lie is necessarily wrong. Or, even if most would agree with the minor premise that traitors are disloyal, it is not at all evident that disloyalty is necessarily a bad thing.

Instead of trying to show that these behaviors are logically wrong, Dante tries to show how painful they are. To the extent that his metaphors seem appropriate, he is demonstrating that to do any of these things is actually a form of suffering. Even if (which we deny) one *could* conclude that flattery, hypocrisy, treachery, bribery, violent temper, and the rest were logical mistakes, one would have to have an uncommon level of commitment to logic to go so far as to suffer if all one seemed to be making was a logical mistake. One consequence of this weakness of logic is revealed by the fact that even acts that are deemed to be clearly illogical (such as randomly killing total strangers) tend to require external sanctions—punishments—in order to deter them.

Here we begin to see the singular force of judgments that can stem from an analysis of the nature of things in themselves rather than from existing premises, whether major or minor, that supposedly apply to them. There is no need to threaten an external punishment in order to make it clear that an action is not worth doing. We say Dante is one who manages such judgments and that he does so by being able to come up with appropriate metaphors for what the things he is analyzing are *like*.

Paradiso

We know, of course, that in the Christian tradition, it is not just that sinners get to be in Hell. Good deeds get us to Heaven. Heaven is supposed to be enjoyable. If Dante is following the same method of analysis to arrive at his version of Heaven that he used to imagine his Hell, now he would be depicting what good deeds are in themselves by imagining what *they* are like. But what these deeds are like would have to be, not just something appropriate to their nature, but also something pleasurable for it to make sense that these acts can put people in Heaven. Given that the acts are, as we shall see, almost inevitably arduous, and frequently even result in early death, it is difficult to see how what it is like to do them can credibly be seen as pleasurable. That Dante does manage to make what various good deeds are like seem enjoyable is what I hope to make clear in this section.

Relatively early in their trip through Paradise, Dante and his guide Beatrice find themselves on the planet Venus. Given its association with the goddess who gave the planet its name, we can anticipate that souls located here will be noteworthy for an interest in love. But, even at the beginning of the Canto, Dante has a way of indicating what, in particular, it is about love that makes him think of some lovers as achieving Paradise. He says that the reason this planet was named after the Goddess of Love is because 'they took the name and gave it to the star which woos the sun at both its nape and brow' (Dante 1986: [c.1321] Canto VIII, ll.11–2, 93).

Barbara Reynolds explains what it is about the planet that Dante is referencing here:

Venus […] is sometimes not visible from earth in the morning because she does not rise until after the sun is above the horizon but she is seen at evening after the sun is set (i.e. she gazes at his nape, following behind him); at other times she sets before the sun and rises before him in the morning (i.e. she gazes on his brow). (Dante 1962: 121, note by Reynolds)

Venus, then, is a very ardent wooer: when she is not busy admiring the sun's nape, it is not that she ceases her admiration. Instead she turns her attention to his brow. Dante is preparing us for persons with a noteworthy interest in the behavior of wooing. And what we do find on this planet are persons famous either for wooing or for their susceptibility to being wooed. In particular, Dante notes the presence here of Cunizza da Romano. She is known particularly, among her numerous other amorous adventures, for abandoning her husband, because she was seduced by the famous troubadour, Sordello (later the subject of a poem by Robert Browning). Cunizza says about herself: 'I was o'ermastered by this planet's flame' (Dante 1962: Canto IX, l.33, 126). Also present is Folquet of Marseille, one of the troubadours and so, we presume, singled out as much for his capacity for wooing as Cunizza is for her capacity for being wooed.

The fate Dante imagines for these and innumerable others greatly swayed by the power of love is to be sparks 'circling' (Dante 1962: Canto IX, l.19, 115) or 'whirling' (Canto IX, l.35, 116) within a great wheel of light. In so doing, they copy Venus herself who, Dante writes, was once believed to have 'whirled radiant, shedding love's madness on the [...] world' (Canto VIII, ll.1–3, 115).

Why does it make sense for them to be spinning around? Perhaps the lyrics of a classic pop song can help here. In 'That Old Black Magic (Johnny Mercer, 1942),' because of love 'I am in a spin, loving that spin I am in.'

Love can put us in a spin. It does seem, then, that being in a spin is a metaphor for what it is like to be mad with love, to be either a troubadour who writes love poems or one highly susceptible to their blandishments. Further, since the song also says we *love* the spin, we have a version not just of what intense love is like but how that (spinning) sensation can be pleasurable. It might be worth mentioning that a more recent song says pretty much the same thing, albeit in more mundane fashion. The group Dead or Alive had a big hit with 'You spin me right round, baby/Right round like a record, baby' (1985).

I suggest, both that Dante has found an appropriate metaphor for what it is like to be a troubadour or to be susceptible to one, and how what this is like can indeed be a form of pleasure, can be, we can say, heavenly.

Leaving Venus, Dante and Beatrice arrive on the Sun. Here they encounter another group of souls. Dante asks us to imagine, concerning these, 'How bright in its own right/Must they have been, which light, /Not colour outlined on the light of/The sun's self' (Dante 1962: Canto X, ll.40–2, 136). These souls are *so* bright that, even without being a different color from the Sun, they are visible against the light of the Sun. In other words, they shine even brighter than the Sun.

That Dante could be imagining lights of such brightness begins to make sense as soon as we learn, via their spokesperson Thomas Aquinas, that this planet is the home of those known for their intellectual power especially, as was Aquinas for clarifying the most profound and vexing religious issues. Like Plato in *The Republic*, then, Dante must be thinking that, as the Sun illuminates the world of material objects, thinkers have been able to shed another kind of light on an even more important world—the world of ideas.

As on the previous planet, the souls here are in a circle, which may lead us to believe that, apart from their exceptional brightness, they are not going to be differentiated from lovers. However, it is worth looking in more detail at the nature of this particular circle. Dante writes that there were 'Many surpassing lights in a bright device, we [he and Beatrice] at the centre, /They as a wreath' (Dante 1962: Canto X, ll.64–5, 137).

So, this time the lights are circling around Dante and Beatrice. Another translator says it is as if they formed a crown around their heads (Dante 1986: Canto X, l.65, 121). And the way the lights are circling also is said to be like the way there is sometimes a halo around the moon (Canto X, l.69, 121).

Unlike in the cases of lovers, then, we are asked to imagine these lights as shining on Dante's head. Also, the lights are not spinning wildly. Finally, and what is probably most important, though Dante says there are many lights we soon learn, thanks to Aquinas who proceeds to identify them, that there are actually only 12. Each of them is a very distinguished scholar. Besides Aquinas and his teacher, Albertus Magnus, there are the venerable Bede, Boethius, and others who, while less well known today, are persons who Dante credits as key figures in his own and his time's intellectual development.

What these figures are imagined as like, it seems fair to say, is a very select circle, a small group of leading lights. It can be suggested that this is both an appropriate image for what it is to be such an accomplished intellectual and, at the same time, to be part of such a circle would certainly be just the sort of fate that people like this would enjoy. Furthermore, even the seemingly odd fact that the lights are hovering just above Dante's head is both appropriate for who they are, i.e. a great influence on how he understands the self-same religious matters that are a major part of the content of the entire *Commedia* and something we can imagine as part of the pleasure of their form of life. As theorists, what could be better than to be a productive influence on someone like Dante?

Arriving on the next planet, Dante 'was aware of having risen higher because I saw the star's candescent smile glow redder than it ever had before' (Dante 1986: Canto XIV, ll.85–7, 171).

From the color, we know he and Beatrice are now on Mars. We can safely assume that this is going to be the home, not of great lovers or great thinkers, but of great warriors. We can also assume that Dante will try to make the warriors appear in some form that shows us what it is like to be one of them. A dazzling thing does appear and Dante's initial description of it certainly does suggest that it is very different from what has presented itself on the previous two planets. First, like Mars it is very red but it is also said to be like a famous natural wonder that is very white. It appears 'just as the Milky Way adorned with stars, some large, some small, gleams white between the Poles, baffling the wisest astrologers' (Dante 1986: Canto XIV, l. 97–9, 171).

The puzzle he is referring to is that what stymied the Ancients about the Milky Way was what sort of body it could be. This interested Dante as well and, in fact, in a previous work, *The Convivio (c.1307)*, he had praised Aristotle for working out the right solution, that it was actually billions of separate stars that produced the effect of one white stripe (Dante 1986: 175, note by Musa).

It can be suggested that we are already beginning to see what being a warrior is like. It is not like being a great thinker, part of a select group, each of whom is easy to distinguish from others. It is instead to be one of a vast number of components, the unity among which is so effective in producing one overall thing that it is not even clear at first that there actually are separate parts that are responsible for making the whole thing. There is also an additional resonance of this image. In a Greek myth that Dante almost certainly would have been familiar with, it is said that the way the Milky Way was formed was by a goddess spilling milk. Just as the goddess produced an impressive white thing by spilling something, the warriors have produced an impressive red thing by spilling something, in their case, blood.

But how is being a warrior as much a source of pleasure as being a great thinker or great lover, as it should be if these souls are actually in Heaven? A further aspect of Dante's metaphor is clearly an attempt to provide an answer to this question. He tells us that *his* Milky Way has a different pattern than the one in nature. What all the innumerable red lights that are the souls of warriors banded together manage to produce is not one stripe but two, intersecting to form a gigantic red cross. Once we learn who, in fact, the warriors by and large are, this image both manages to be an even more precise version of what it is like to have been one of these warriors and also provides a convincing sense of how they might well take pleasure in their actions, including even in their deaths. What is revealed is that they are not just warriors but, mostly, warriors who took part in the Crusades. What they did, i.e. defended Christianity, was *like* a way of helping the cross keep its shape and, certainly, if what they did was like this, it would be a great source of pleasure for them.

Dante and Beatrice next arrive on a planet described as 'of sheen pure white' (Dante 1962: Canto XVIII, ll.67–8, 216). Based on Ptolemy's astronomy, we know this must be Jupiter. Since Venus was the home of lovers and Mars of warriors, Jupiter is likely to be reserved for kings. However, it remains to be seen what sort of kings achieve Heaven. As happened on Mars, the souls again arrive in a shape that reminds Dante of a remarkable natural phenomenon, in this case not the Milky Way but how flocks of birds sometimes form, in flight, a letter of the alphabet, usually V. But these 'birds' do more than that. First they spell out, letter by letter, an entire Latin sentence. Then the last letter of the sentence, which happens to be an M, turns into a giant figure of the bird that arguably an M already looks a bit like: an eagle at rest.

Assuming that to become like an eagle is to become a worthy king, watching over the earth eagle-like, Dante's idea would seem to be that the lives of those who end up in this part of Heaven are managing to be *like* a set of letters that, taken together, spell out something that can produce a message of what it is to be a worthy king. Everything then depends on what the letters say. It turns out that what they are spelling out is 'love justice, ye that judge the earth' (Dante 1986: Canto XVIII, ll.91–3, 216; as translated by Mark Musa on page 220). In confirmation that the souls who are placed here can indeed be said to convey this message, it is the case that what all six of those whose identity we learn have in common, even including the one of them who was not actually a king,[1] is that they are noteworthy for a commitment to justice.

It also seems evident that, particularly for someone who in life was a king, being a contributor to a message that spells out what just rule requires is not only a plausible version of what one's life was like. Such a fate would also surely be a source of great pleasure for such a person.

Now Dante and Beatrice arrive on the last planet they will visit. Beatrice explains that they have been lifted to 'the seventh light' (Dante 1986: Canto XXI, l.13, 248). According to Ptolemy's astronomy this is Saturn, named after Jupiter's father, who was said to have ushered in a very rare thing for Rome, a 'golden era' of peace. We can guess that the souls who have gotten themselves here will be known for their peaceful form of existence but, to be worthy of Heaven, it will surely have to be a form of peace that is not merely dull.

Even though they are already on the planet that (again according to Ptolemy) places them higher above the earth than any other, what appears to Dante makes it evident that it is possible to go still higher: 'Coloured like gold which flashes back the light/I saw a ladder raised aloft so far/It soared beyond the compass of my sight' (Dante 1962, Canto XXI, ll.28–30, 242).

The souls are on various rungs, whizzing up and down the ladder. One soul flies down to the bottom of the ladder to speak to Dante, explaining, before he identifies himself, that the reason he shines so brightly is because, climbing or really whizzing up the ladder 'Lifts me above myself until I gaze/Upon His essence' (Dante 1962: Canto XXI, ll.86–7, 243).

Like us, Dante is curious to know whom he is speaking to. Reynolds explains:

This is the soul of St. Peter Damian. Born of a humble family in Ravenna […] he entered the monastery of Fonte Ovellano […] he became an Abbot. Much against his will, he was created Cardinal and Bishop of Ostia in 1058. (Dante 1962: 246, note by Reynolds)

We suspect that the souls here are known for their monastic existence. Any remaining doubts are removed—both as to what in particular about his career has landed Peter Damian on this planet and what has given him the fate of being able to whizz up and down a golden ladder—when we discover that the only other person Dante converses with on Saturn is St Benedict himself, 'the founder of Monasticism in the Western Church' (Dante 1962: 254, note by Reynolds). It is not hard to intuit ourselves that Dante is imagining this form of life as *like* having a ladder to Heaven. Furthermore, he has St Benedict authorize this, first by saying that the monastic life is the way in which 'the power to rise above on man is confirmed' (Canto XXII, l.42, 250) and second, even more directly, by making reference to St Benedict's own book of monastic rules (c.530) in which *he* used the same image of a ladder to Heaven as what the monastic life can offer. With the only difference being that, in this case, he does not even need to invent the image himself, Dante has, as with lovers, scholars, warriors, and just kings, again arrived at what is a highly appropriate metaphor for what it is like to live this particular sort of life and, at the same time, at a heavenly pleasure for the people concerned.

The judgments that Dante arrives at which place people in Paradise are even less likely to be possible as products of syllogisms than those he reaches in the Inferno. For example, even if one can imagine proving logically that the kind of wisdom Dante puts such a positive evaluation on is a good thing, that would not be the same as being able to specify, as does Dante, what makes it so good. And if logic is so limited in its ability to judge wisdom's quality, it is surely even less feasible that it could help us visualize the merits of love.

Purgatorio

Christian theology also offers a third option, Purgatory. Dorothy Sayers struggles to specify the difference between how Dante treats this place and how he treats Hell: 'The pains of Purgatory are in themselves very like those of Hell, and some of them are but little lighter. The penitent Proud, like the impenitent Hypocrites ceaselessly walk their appointed rounds bowed down by heavy weights' (Dante 1955: 15, note by Sayers).

She is referring to the first cornice of Purgatory in which Dante and his companion, here Virgil rather than Beatrice, see a group so stooped over by the burden of the heavy stones they carry on their backs that, when they spot them, Dante and Virgil are not even sure they are seeing human beings.

Sayers is surely right that these persons' suffering seems quite as bad as having to trudge around in a gold coat lined with lead but, whereas it is clear that the coat is a metaphor for hypocrisy, it is not at all clear what, if anything, being bent over by a stone is like. It certainly does not seem *like* pride.

In order to resolve Sayers's confusion as to the Purgatory–Hell distinction, it will be helpful to look at Dante's and Virgil's experiences on this cornice in more detail. When they arrive, they see three very lifelike white marble statues. The first portrays the Annunciation. The second shows the Old Testament's King David bowing down before the Holy Ark while his wife laughs at him for behaving in a manner not becoming for a king. The third shows another ruler, the Roman emperor Trajan, stopping his entire army to take the time to listen to and even respond sympathetically to the grief of a poor widow. We might already guess what the common theme of these statues is but Dante goes so far as to actually tell us directly. We are seeing 'the image of the great humilities' (Dante 1955 [c.1315]: Canto X, l.97, 146).

Being bent over by weights is not like what the proud do but it is *like* what Mary, David, and Trajan do: they are humble enough to shoulder burdens, burdens that could be said to be beneath their dignity, even humiliating. If, as I shall argue, what the metaphor depicts— not the bad thing that the sinners on the cornice are guilty of, but the good thing that they need to learn to do—is typical of how Dante formulates the fates in Purgatory, we have the essential difference between the two places. As Sayers notices, it is not that those in Purgatory do not experience pain. But the difference is that they experience, not pointless pain but worthwhile pain. It is pain that shows, metaphorically, the precise virtue that they need to learn in order to move on; in the case of these too proud people on the first cornice, humility.

Dante and Virgil arrive on the second cornice. Based on their previous experience, an initial puzzle is that there are no statues on this cornice pointing to what the sinners placed here must learn. Instead they hear voices communicating three stories: Jesus' mother, Mary, being upset because the guests at a wedding have run out of wine; Orestes and his great friend Pylades trying to die in each other's place; and, finally, Jesus suggesting that we should love our enemies. At this point, Virgil concludes: 'This circle doth reprove and scourge the sin of envy; that is why its whip is fashioned from the cords of love' (Dante 1955: Canto XIII, ll.37–9, 167).

It is certainly right that we have been told three stories of persons devoid of envy but the idea of 'love' is quite imprecise as a version of the good thing that the envious need to learn.

Here it helps to examine the case of Sapia, one of the sinners who is being purged on this cornice. She says about herself, in what amounts to a precise statement of the mistake of envy: 'My heart conceived more joy from others' loss than my own gain' (Dante 1955: Canto XIII, ll.110–1, 169).

Equally relevant is the fact that one of the (envious) voices heard on this cornice is the cry: 'Behold, now, everyone that findeth me shall slay me' (Dante 1955: Canto XIV, ll.133–4, 177). This is Cain's cry, as reported in Genesis, when God banishes him for killing Abel. We can gather from both Sapia's story and Cain's, that the specific good that the envious need to learn is too vaguely formulated as love. It is to learn to concentrate just on themselves and to do so, in particular, by not paying so much attention to other people.

The metaphor for what the envious need to learn, not yet mentioned, now seems completely appropriate. Dante has the sinners on this cornice suffering by having their eyes stitched shut. We can remark that this is a good metaphor both for what it would be particularly painful for these people to have to do and what it would be really good for them to learn to do.

In an early indication that, on the third cornice as well, the penitents will not have full use of their eyes, before he makes contact with them Dante is again given three good examples, but this time in the form of mental visions that come to him. First he witnesses Mary responding not with the strong rebuke that might seem justified but 'a mother's tender gesture' to the incident when Jesus, at the age of 12, went missing for three whole days (Dante 1955: Canto XV, l.89, 183). Then, he has a vision of the Greek tyrant Pisistratus resisting his wife's call for vengeance with an 'unruffled mien' (Canto XV, l.102, 184) and, finally, he sees the Old Testament figure, Stephen, even as he is being stoned by an angry mob, imploring God to pardon his enemies.

From what has happened on the first two cornices, we expect that these stories will share a theme that can teach the specific lesson that the sinners placed here need to learn. At this point a cloud of smoke comes rolling toward Virgil and Dante, 'so black that one's eyes could not keep open' (Dante 1955: Canto XVI, l.7, 188). The fate of the souls on this cornice is to try to find their way about though, as one of those placed here tells Dante: 'the smoke has made us blind' (Canto XVI, l.35, 189). Virgil explains that the souls here 'go loosening the knot of wrath that held them thrall' (Canto XVI, ll.23–4, 188). The smoke then, is *like* the anger that could have gotten the better of Mary, Pisistratus, and Stephen.

It becomes even clearer what being able to find their way through the smoke is like and why to do so is a valuable lesson when, just before leaving the cornice, Dante gets three more visions: He sees Procne getting so angry with her husband for his adultery that she kills her own son and tricks her husband into eating him; Hamon trying to get every Jew in Persia killed just because he felt insulted by one of them; and Amata making the mistake of thinking her daughter's fiancé had been killed in battle and getting so angry she kills herself. These would all be people who have not managed to stop themselves being blinded by the smoke.

Arriving on the next cornice, Dante tells us that 'I bent my ear to the new circuit's rim/To see if any sound would issue thence' (Dante 1955: Canto XVII, ll.79–80, 198).

It seems that, having gotten used to forms of sin that block vision, he now expects the new group of sinners to have to hear rather than see their lesson. However, there seem to be no external stimuli of any kind and, in their absence, Dante proceeds to fall asleep. What happens next both wakes Dante and begins to explain why this cornice has such a different environment. The sinners here don't have the time to stop to look or even to listen: 'When all at once, and close behind our backs/Startling me up, a throng came roundabout [...] The whole great crowd were running at top speed' (Dante 1955: Canto XVIII, ll.88–98, 207–8).

The puzzle we have as to what good behavior the souls need to learn, and what good behavior could be like learning not to stop running, is resolved as soon as we hear what the lead runners are shouting.[2] They cry: 'Mary ran to the hills in haste' (Dante 1955: Canto XVIII, l.100, 208). And then: 'Caesar, to subjugate Ilerda/Thrust hard at Marseille and raced on into Spain' (Canto XVIII, ll.101–2, 208).

The first cry refers to the story of Mary's reaction to the Annunciation. Gabriel, in order to convince her that God was indeed capable of impregnating her, points out that He had already done something similar to her cousin Elizabeth. What is impressing the sinners in the story in the Gospel of Luke is that Mary did not delay. She *hastened* to see Elizabeth to confirm Gabriel's claim. Similarly, Caesar too is noteworthy for not delaying. He did not wait until he defeated one city before attacking another. Instead he left part of his army to complete the job while he led the rest into Spain.

Both Mary and Caesar can be said to have a highly developed sense of urgency and we can say developing such a sense of urgency is both what these sinners need to learn[3] and that developing such a sense is *like* learning to run as fast as one possibly can.

Arriving on the fifth cornice, Dante and Virgil find 'people stretched out [...] weeping, their faces turned toward the ground' (Dante 1955: Canto XIX, ll.71–2, 218).

Compared to being forced to carry huge stones on one's back, having one's eyes stitched shut, being surrounded by thick black smoke, and even having to run at full speed, this fate does not seem all that painful, so our first problem is to get clearer on why this is actually a form of suffering and even one that makes one of the cornice's souls say: 'The mount has no more bitter pain than this' (Dante 1955: Canto XIX, l.117, 219).

Dante reports that, as they face the ground, the souls are sighing: 'my soul cleaveth to the dust' (Sayers 222, l.73, 218). The reference is to an Old Testament psalm. (Psalms 119) Obviously, Dante has derived the treatment of these souls from this source but, more importantly, the sentiment expressed in the psalm begins to suggest what might be painful about facing the ground. The position could be a metaphor for not being able to focus on *spiritual* fulfillment.

And we soon learn how appropriate this metaphor is for depicting what the lives of the people placed here have been like. Dante first meets a pope and then a king, both of whom express regret at being consumed by worldly ambition. Furthermore, the metaphor becomes even more appropriate and their pain even clearer when one of them reveals that they are actually tied to the ground, unable to move. But while the worldly focus that they can now see as like a form of suffering could cure them of a desire for worldly success, how does being tied to the ground also, as we claim all the fates in Purgatory do, hint at a positive alternative?

In this regard it is worth examining in some detail what the king is doing and saying when Dante encounters him:

> Then, just ahead, by hap I heard one fling a cry out: 'Ah, sweet Mary.' Such a moan as of a woman travailing. 'How poor thou wast we know' the voice went on, 'Seeing to what hostel thou didst bring thy precious and blissful burden, there to lay it down.' (Dante 1955: Canto XX, ll.19–24, 224)

While, at first glance, it seems a far-fetched association to make, we can presume that the fact that he is lying tethered on the ground makes him identify with Mary, deprived of a bed and therefore forced to give birth to Jesus in a stable. If this is the event that his pain can help him to understand the significance of, then clearly, like the sinners on other cornices, his suffering too has a positive outcome.

And as he tells Dante more of his story, additional reasons besides his current position that explain why he would be stimulated to think about how Jesus was born come to the surface. First, it is revealed that he, too, as it were, gave birth to something. He says: 'Of the malignant tree was I the root whose shade so blights all Christian lands that small their harvest is of any wholesome fruit' (Dante 1955: Canto XX, ll.43–5, 225).

Sayers tells us that he means that he was 'founder of the Capetian dynasty of the kings of France (who) [...] exercised a dominating influence throughout Europe for some two and a half centuries. Many of Dante's most virulent hatreds attach to members of this family' (Dante 1955: 229, note by Sayers). So, as Mary gave birth to something very good, he gave birth to something very bad.

Furthermore, the way Mary gave birth (which he dwells on) even has a specific resonance for this king. It is likely that he is so inspired by the fact that Mary did not mind giving birth in a stable, i.e. a place reserved for animals, because it directly contrasts with what must be the oddest feature of his own life story. He tells Dante that 'a Paris butcher sired me' (Dante 1955: Canto XX, l.52, 225). That fulfilling the form of ambition that he now bemoans required an escape from his own originally close ties to animals, must make the fact of where Mary did *not* need to escape from in order to deliver Jesus, a compelling reminder of the route to the new type of fulfillment his position is teaching him to appreciate.

On the next cornice Dante and Virgil see a strange fruit tree: 'As a fir tree tapers from the top […] so this one tapers down' (Dante 1955: Canto XXII, ll.133–4, 244). A voice in it calls out: 'Ye shall be famished of this food' (Canto XXII, l.141, 244). We gather that the reason the tree has this shape is to stop the souls on this cornice from being able to reach the fruit. In the same vein, there is also a stream of water to which there is no possible access.

That there is this food and drink but no way to eat or drink it is confirmed by the fact that, while the man he first encounters on this cornice is Forese Donati, said to have been Dante's best friend, he is now so thin that Dante only can recognize him by his voice. When Forese explains that the problem of the souls placed here is 'excessive greed of life's good things' (Dante 1955: Canto XXIII, l. 65, 249), on the one hand it seems quite appropriate that they need to get thin but, on the other hand, it could seem that, unlike the souls on all the other cornices, what they are having to deal with is more like a straightforward punishment, i.e. starvation, than a metaphor for what their sin is and how they might remedy it.

In fact, this is how Sayers interprets the inaccessible food and water. The souls, because of 'over-indulgence in bodily comforts,' are 'accordingly purged by starvation within sight of plenty' (Dante 1955: 251, note by Sayers). In this interpretation, it is hard to see both how the tree and water and the souls' relation to them are a metaphor for anything and how the over-indulgent are being shown any sort of way forward.

On the other cornices, the meaning of the sinners' fate sometimes became much clearer once we knew more about the sinners themselves. Justifying an action that would otherwise seem rude by explaining: 'No reason why I should not here name each at thy demand since our starved features are so shrunk and dry' (Dante 1955: Canto XXIV, ll.16–9, 254).

Forese identifies a series of his fellow sufferers who, it has to be said, are so guilty of this sin as to be figures of fun. For example, there is the Pope who died from eating too many of a special delicacy: 'eels from the lake of Bolsena, stewed in Vernaccia wine' (Dante 1955: 259, note by Sayers). There is the relative of a distinguished family of clergy but whose only personal claim to fame is that 'he had a great knack for inventing new culinary recipes' (259, note by Sayers). There is Lord Marchese, 'a renowned drinker from Foli' (260, note by Sayers).

What is stimulating about realizing that it is people like these who are placed here is that, in their actual lives, they would have been very unlikely to have agreed with Sayers that it is 'plenty' they are being starved 'within sight of.' Fruit and water are not plenty to someone partial to Bolsena eels stewed in wine. As a longing for fruit and water would be a new experience for people like this, we can say that it is more that they are being taught to *want* these things than being punished by being deprived of them. As such, we can conclude that they are being given a version of what it would be good for a former glutton to become, i.e. someone who would be content just with fruit and water, and a version of what a glutton is *like*, i.e. someone who does not appreciate what Sayers takes for granted, namely that fruit and water, is, while it might pain them to admit it, indeed enough, and so, at least in one sense of the word, plenty.

Arriving on the seventh and last cornice, Dante and Virgil find a sort of fiery furnace: 'The bank belches forth great sheets of flame while upward from the cornice edge does blow a blast that shields it, backward bending them' (Dante 1955: Canto XXV, ll.112–4, 266).

Walking carefully single file to avoid the flames, first they hear souls within the flame crying: 'I know not man' (Dante 1955: Canto XXV, l.128, 266). The reference is to what Mary told the angel when Gabriel announced that she was pregnant. Next, the souls refer to the myth in which the virgin Diana expelled one of her followers from her group because this girl got pregnant.

We guess that the souls placed here will have issues somehow connected with sex but it is quite unclear what this might have to do with needing to endure a fiercely burning fire. The soul who begins speaking to Dante explains that this cornice is for those who 'like brute beasts were slaves to appetite' (Dante 1955: Canto XXVI, l.84, 274). Based on this and similar statements, Sayers decides that what this cornice is purging is 'lust' (267, note by Sayers). However, once we know the identity of the person Dante is speaking with, we can begin to suspect that the focus, while it probably includes lust, is actually much more specific. Dante discovers his interlocutor is Guido Guinicelli whom he identifies as 'father to me and to my betters—all who use love's own sweet style and chivalrous' (Canto XXVI, ll.98–9, 274).

In other words, Guido is the poet who most influenced Dante in his early *Vita Nuova* *(c.1294)* phase, when he too was a love poet. That it is the love poets rather than the more straightforwardly lustful who are most in need of and/or most likely to benefit from whatever the fire is meant to accomplish is confirmed by the fact that the only other souls Guido identifies are Arnault Daniel and Guido d'Arrezzo, two more and perhaps even greater love poets than Guido himself or the young Dante.

Returning to the fact that the fire they are enduring seems a kind of furnace, it can be suggested, as Sayers probably senses by the biblical passage she cites in trying to interpret what the fire is doing, that what the fire must be doing is *refining* love (Dante 1955: 267, note by Sayers). As an image of what love poetry is, it would mean that such poetry is not sufficiently refined. As an image of what is needed, what is being recommended is more refinement.

Concerning what refined love or a refined love poet might look like, it is worth noting that this is the only cornice on which Dante himself is purged. Understandably, he is very reluctant to walk through a fiery furnace. What finally persuades him is when Virgil says: 'Look my son […] Twixt Beatrice and thee there is this wall' (Dante 1955: Canto XXVII, ll.35–6, 282). He needs to go through the fire because it is *like* the refinement of love that is needed before he can meet Beatrice in Paradise. That is, in terms of Dante's career, while he already had love for Beatrice, as expressed in *his* love poem, the *Vita Nuova*, what can and does happen when that love is refined is that, while Beatrice is still his love, now that love inspires not mere love poems but the whole *Divine Comedy*. Finally, it is worth noting that going through a fire to refine love is quite a precise metaphor for this transformation from one kind of poet to another, because the difference between his feelings for Beatrice in the two works is not at all that his love for her is replaced in the later book by something else. It really is as if it is *refined*.

That Dante can show what in particular all these sinners need to learn is another aspect of his accomplishment that would not be possible were he committed to syllogisms. For a syllogism to be able to conclude that one would benefit from these treatments, it would need to *assume* that these various forms of action are bad and that certain alternatives are good, whereas Dante, by developing a way to visualize humility, refined love, urgency, etc. is actually helping us to understand what actually *is* bad about the corresponding sins and therefore good about overcoming them.

In analyzing the three parts of the *Divine Comedy* we have necessarily emphasized the different approaches Dante must take to satisfy the different requirements for earning a place in Hell, Purgatory, and Heaven. However, that should not be allowed to obscure what all three books have in common. He is always finding a similarity that is not immediately apparent. In Hell things that at first appear to be attractive turn out to be like things that are not at all attractive. For example, flattering others looks an attractive option until we see how close it is to letting dung come out of our mouths. In Heaven, things that at first do not look attractive end up seeming so. For example, living in a monastery may well seem boring until we see its likeness to having a ladder to heaven. In Purgatory, matters are more complicated because he must show both that the sin is not as attractive as it appears and also that the punishment is not as awful as *it* appears. For example, in seeing that a more moderate life is like one in which one would actually crave fruit and water, the Bolsena eel lover is seeing both that he was too greedy (because he did not long for things like fruit and water) and that it would not be so terrible to not be so greedy (because of what he could still have and even want). In all the books, then, Dante manages to enlighten us as to the identity of activities, e.g. flattery, the monastic life, moderation, by developing metaphors for them.

Notes

1   The one person who was not a king is a character in the *Aeneid (c.19 BC)* who Virgil singles out for how just he is (Dante 1986: 243, note by Musa).
2   Not being allowed to stop, look, and listen to get their lessons, they shout them out themselves while running.
3   No commentator has actually been able to identify the souls on this cornice as noteworthy for sloth, so in this case the conclusion has the status of what we can safely assume from Dante's overall method.

Chapter 2

Metaphor in Fairy Tales

While I do think Dante is exceptional in his ability to use metaphors to analyze phenomena, it would be foolish in the extreme to treat him as unique. In this chapter, the use of metaphors by some other authors will be explored. In particular, Bruno Bettelheim's idea that fairy tales are more realistic than they seem will be interpreted as depending on the metaphoric content of these works. Furthermore, as we saw with Dante, it will be suggested that the metaphors in fairy tales that we identify take the form of judgments.

A wolf tries to disguise itself as one's grandmother. A young woman lives for a time in a state of reasonable contentment with a bunch of dwarfs. A suffering person finally achieves a happy life just because a shoe fits. A beast is changed into a handsome human.

We recognize these events as parts of the plots of some of the most well-known and well-loved fairy tales. If we say that all of these stories are unrealistic, we presumably mean that all these events cannot happen. Bettelheim, surely the person who has done the most to revive our interest in fairy tales, formulates these stories' lack of realism as the fact that they contain instances of magic, of enchantment. One dictionary definition of enchantment is 'to put under a spell or endow with magical powers' (Clarendon Press 1993). The stories are unrealistic in that they endow the world—life—with magical powers. They portray things that could only happen if the world did not obey the laws of science, laws according to which beasts do not suddenly become human; gangs of dwarfs do not live in forests while looking after young girls; etc.

Thus far it could seem sufficient simply to conclude that these stories have nothing to do with real life. But Bettelheim also says that the stories have an affinity with enchantment in another sense: they have the power to enchant children. This usage is in keeping with another dictionary definition of enchantment. To enchant is to 'charm, delight, enrapture' (Clarendon Press 1993).

No one can disagree with Bettelheim's first point—that fairy tales portray instances of enchantment. Most would also agree with his second point—that the stories can enchant children. Surely, for example, the success of the various early Disney movies is a demonstration of this. However, the dictionary also offers a third meaning of enchantment. To enchant can be 'to delude' (Clarendon Press 1993). Many object to fairy tales precisely on the grounds that they merely pedal a delusion.[1] Since we are unlikely to have our lives changed forever just because a shoe fits us, much less face a wolf disguised as one's grandmother, it is misleading to portray any such thing. It is here that Bettelheim strongly disagrees. He thinks that fairy tales provide valuable, even essential, lessons.

Where his argument is hard to pin down, though, is why he disagrees with those opposed to fairy tales. He says that the reason why such stories are valuable is because they provide the optimism and encouragement children need. But, at times, Bettelheim seems to suggest that the stories can only manage to do this by misleading the child. That is, the stories are misleading in the (good?) way that Plato recommends telling 'noble lies' to the young. An overly rosy representation of reality is recommended until children are old enough to accept the much harsher truth. But such a view is vulnerable to the familiar charge that fairy tales do not prepare one to face reality. They give one unrealistic expectations, e.g. of a marriage that will be happy *forever* rather than have ups and downs.

At other times, Bettelheim offers an at once more interesting but also seemingly harder to defend view. Without ever saying this directly, he can certainly at various points be read as saying that, actually, fairy tales are not as unrealistic as they appear. But that takes us back to our initial question: How can stories that contain either impossible or highly improbable events be said to be realistic? Baldly put, if there are events that are quite probable in real life that can be *compared* to things that could only happen by magic, then it is possible after all for what can't happen (the magical event) to offer a credible interpretation of what can happen.

I would suggest that it is possible to find likely real-life events that justify the authors' interpretations of them as having a magical quality in the case of all the stories with which this chapter began. An attempted seduction *is* like being lured into bed by a wolf that tries to pretend that what will ensue is as harmless as getting into bed with one's grandmother. Finding yourself living a reasonably contented but yet overly narrow life in which one would never fulfill one's considerable potential *is* like living with a bunch of dwarfs. Finding recognition for one's real qualities *is* like getting what one wants out of life merely by being able to fit into a shoe. That there are endless possibilities for revising our views of the apparently hostile suggests that beasts really can change their appearance. Fairy tales then, like the *Divine Comedy*, can be seen as about reality in the way any good metaphor can be about reality—by helping us to see what aspects of reality are like.

Although it is certainly true that Bettelheim deserves to be seen as the source for the argument that fairy tales develop credible ways to understand real events, he never quite achieves full clarity on this point or so I now will try to show.

Turning first to his analysis of 'Little Red Riding Hood,' while he believes, no doubt rightly, that the story is about seduction rather than the danger of being eaten by a wolf ('the wolf is the seducer' [Bettelheim 1991: 170]), still, he says: 'The hearer of the story rightly wonders why the wolf does not devour Little Red Cap as soon as he meets her—that is, at the first opportunity' (174–5).

As it would, of course, not be possible for the wolf to put on a disguise if he ate the girl straight away, we can already see that Bettelheim is not attributing much significance to the wolf needing not to appear as he really is. And, though it is true that he then says that the wolf's behavior in not eating Little Red Riding Hood straight away 'begins to make sense if we assume that to get to Little Red Cap, the wolf had to do away with Grandmother' (Bettelheim 1991: 175) he does not see the wolf's motivation here as the obvious one of needing to hide in the grandmother's clothes. Instead we get a convoluted Oedipal explanation in which the grandmother becomes a substitute mother and the wolf, while still a seducer, now is somehow also the girl's father:

> As long as the (grand)mother is around, Little Red Cap will not become his. But once the (grand)mother is out of the way, the road seems open for acting on one's desires which had to remain repressed as long as Mother was around. The story on this level deals with the daughter's unconscious wish to be seduced by her father (the wolf). (Bettelheim 1991: 175)

And even though he notes that in fact when Little Red Riding Hood arrives at her grandmother's house she 'is confused by the wolf's having disguised himself in the old woman's attire' (Bettelheim 1991: 172), he still does not see that the disguise would not have been possible if the wolf had eaten the girl straight away. What otherwise seems an inexplicable blindness on Bettelheim's part makes much more sense if what he does not appreciate is that the story is not just about a seduction but is attempting to suggest what a seduction is like and, furthermore, that it manages to suggest that it is not just like being approached by a wolf (which of course, while a possible metaphor, has become something of a cliché) but by a wolf disguised as one's grandmother. This would accomplish two things that Bettelheim probably does not see the story doing: develop the magic-like quality of this event and illuminate what seduction is like.

When a metaphor has become a cliché, since it is not the case that the resemblance it is based on has become inappropriate, why has it lost at least some of its illuminating power? Metaphors, as we have emphasized, are an aesthetic tool and so a way to see why, when they become over-familiar, they lose some of their cogency is to grasp the form that aesthetic understanding takes. Aesthetic understanding is different from *automatic* understanding:

> Those enactments of understanding are termed automatic that make use of conventions to successfully identify the object to be understood; on the other hand, non-automatic enactments of understanding are those that consist solely in the process of identification, without the support of conventions. (Menke 1998: 31)

When a metaphor becomes a cliché—when we grasp its meaning—what goes on is more like automatic understanding than this aesthetic mode of identifying a thing. 'Wolf,' for example, has become just a sign that the conventions dictate means seducer—is virtually a synonym of it—rather than an apparently very different thing that, when and if we can see what it is similar to, we come to understand something of the nature of that thing, in this case the thing being a seducer.

Turning to 'Snow White,' where the limitation of Bettelheim's approach most clearly surfaces is in his interpretation of the significance of the dwarfs. In general, it certainly seems right to suggest that 'it is the years Snow White spends with the dwarfs which stand for her times of troubles, of working through problems, her period of growth' (Bettelheim 1991: 201).

However, what exactly does he think the troubles and problems are and in what sense does she need to grow? As he points out, with the dwarfs she 'lives a peaceful existence for a while' (Bettelheim 1991: 208), which raises the question of what could be wrong with living a peaceful life. Bettelheim goes on to tell us, quoting from the actual story, what form this life takes:

> This is what the dwarfs request of her for living with them: she can remain with them and lack nothing if 'You will take care of our household, cook, make the beds, wash, sew and knit, and will keep everything clean and in good order.' (Bettelheim 1991: 208)

Clearly, what becomes crucial is what we are to make of this form of life that, as we now know, living with dwarfs requires of one. What it means to Bettelheim is that 'Snow White becomes a good housekeeper, as is true of many a young girl who, with her mother away, takes good care of her father, the house, and even her siblings' (Bettelheim 1991: 208).

Even though, in fact, young girls sometimes do have to do all this, it is extremely peculiar that Bettelheim starts talking about these tasks as distinctive to young girls. After all and much more typically, they have been what traditional mothers have had to do since time immemorial. The explanation for why Bettelheim sees it this way is because, as with 'Little Red Riding Hood,' he is again seeking traces of things Oedipal. That is, he sees Snow White as unconsciously seeking to replace her (step)mother in her father's affections.

By seeing it this way, even though Snow White is doing quite grown up things, Bettelheim can still argue that her problem is that she is not grown up yet. That is, she is an adolescent—a 'pubertal girl'—immature. He then tries to interpret the dwarfs in a way that fits into this picture. He sees them as 'failing to develop into mature humanity' or, in the same vein, that they 'symbolize an immature, pre-individual, form of existence' (Bettelheim 1991: 200).

But, whether one sees this from the perspective of what a housewife is or from the perspective of what a dwarf is, his interpretation seems deeply flawed. There may be plenty of things wrong with being a housewife but is immaturity really an illuminating way to visualize this state? And while dwarfs are small, they actually are examples of mature humanity, but mature humanity that is not able to grow any more. If being a housewife is like this, then it would be in the sense that, even though one is a grown up, one is not allowed to grow anymore. One is living in an overly restricted environment; one's horizons are too confined, too narrow.[2]

I would again attribute Bettelheim's failure to appreciate the force of a metaphor to a lack of clarity as to what the story's author, at his or her best, is managing to do, i.e. actually help us again to visualize in this case both what it is like to live a narrow existence (such as but not only as a housewife) and also how such an existence has a magical quality. In both of these respects, the author tells us it is because such a life is like a life among dwarfs.

Bettelheim writes that 'by all accounts "Cinderella" is the best-known fairy tale, and probably also the best-liked' (Bettelheim 1991: 236). However, in order to account for its enduring appeal, he believes he must resist what he considers a merely superficial reading of it: 'On the surface, "Cinderella" […] tells about the agonies of sibling rivalry, of wishes coming true, of the humble being elevated, of true merit being recognized […] of virtue rewarded and evil punished—a straightforward story' (239).

Bettelheim thinks none of these themes are of sufficient value or interest to warrant the story's classic status. While this is an issue to which we will need to return, first it is worth considering how he can argue that 'Cinderella' is *not* a story of a virtuous person being rewarded by having her merit recognized.

His idea is that Cinderella is not really as good as the text makes her appear, nor are her stepsisters so evil. In order to sustain this, on the face of it, peculiar reading, he utilizes his by now familiar Oedipal theme: Cinderella is no virtuous innocent because what the story is really about is her wish to eliminate her siblings in order to become the sole object of her father's affections (Bettelheim 1991: 239ff.).

However, there is no way Bettelheim can sustain this interpretation without showing how it is congruent with the story's ending and most memorable image, the slipper that fits only Cinderella. He attempts to argue that the slipper is a 'symbol' of the fact that Cinderella has transcended the Oedipal stage. Rather like (in his version) Snow White, she has become mature, here in the sense that she is now ready for sexual intercourse with someone other than her father. The slipper fitting becomes a symbol for normal sexual intercourse (Bettelheim 1991: 269ff.).

While, as they surely do, both this interpretation of the ending and the re-evaluation of Cinderella's moral character seem forced, developing an alternative to Bettelheim's reading requires engaging with his initial sense that the 'straightforward' version of the story makes it seem banal. What Bettelheim probably means is that ideas such as wishes coming true, merit being recognized, and virtue rewarded seem mere fantasy, thus managing to reveal nothing valuable or interesting about the actual possibilities of life. He does seem to have a point because getting everything one ever wished for certainly does seem an unrealistic aspiration. However, Cinderella, arguably, has the much more modest wish that her merits and her stepsisters' demerits come to light. While, alas, even this is not necessarily a feature of real life, there is a *real* fact that makes it not all that improbable. Hiding demerits is not as easy as it could seem because it requires pretence, distorting who one is and what one does. On the other hand, if one really has merits, no such pretence is necessarily required for the merits to appear because they fit with who you actually are and what you have actually done.

As such, what Bettelheim refers to as 'a very strange incident which takes place in most versions of Cinderella […] the stepsisters mutilation of their feet to make them fit the tiny slipper' (Bettelheim 1991: 267) now appears as a stimulating way to visualize (by comparison) the contortions one will be compelled to embark on in so far as one does not wish one's really existing demerits to be recognized. Similarly, the ease with which Cinderella can slip into the shoe manages to visualize the fact that if one does have actual merits, no such contortions may be required on one's part to make them appear.

Following on from this analysis, one suggestion as to why 'Cinderella' may be the best-loved fairy tale is because, with this central comparison of having a shoe fit (or not) to being recognized for who one is, it manages to do more than the other stories we have discussed. Besides helping us to visualize a real phenomenon, it also demonstrates how something we could wish for may not be as impossible as it could seem. At the same time, as do the other stories, it endows an aspect of real life with a magical—an enchanted—quality. In this instance what is like magic, enchanting, is that getting what one wished for can be like something as mundane as finding a shoe that fits.

Admittedly, this sense of wonder may be somewhat diminished for those who associate the ending with the cliché 'if the shoe fits wear it' because, as said above, comparisons must not seem too obvious if they are to retain their full force. However, if we appreciate that the fate of Cinderella and her stepsisters is *not* like everyone being able to find a shoe that fits but like the *same* (desirable) shoe being an impossible fit for some no matter how hard they try, while also not just a possible but a perfect fit for another without their having to try hard at all. As such, the comparison manages both a more positive and more illuminating message about what can be required to get some desired fate than the cliché would suggest, namely both that one may not need to force it and that it may actually be impossible to force it.

Can we get clearer on what keeps Bettelheim from seeing the metaphoric status of these and other stories? Central is his assumption that fairy tales deal in what he calls symbols.[3] Particularly in the detailed analyses in the second half of his book where, as we have seen, he insists the stories have Oedipal themes, he treats the stories as symbolic in the way orthodox psychoanalysts do: 'There is general agreement that fairy tales speak to us in the language of symbols representing unconscious symbolic content' (Bettelheim 1991: 36). For example, the wolf in 'Little Red Riding Hood' is a symbol of a male seducer. Or, and much more problematically, when the father in 'Beauty and the Beast' brings Beauty back the rose she requested, 'his doing so symbolizes both his love for her and also an anticipation of her losing her maidenhood, as the broken flower—particularly the rose—is a symbol for the loss of virginity' (306).

Besides finding symbols of this sort, less frequently Bettelheim also argues that the stories are symbolic in another sense. He says that children, like primitive people, i.e. those who lack the form of understanding that comes from 'modern science' (Bettelheim 1991: 47), tend to take as 'literally true [what] […] is only a symbol' (50). His example is the way the ancient Egyptians 'symbolize' heaven and the sky. He writes that they see these 'as a mother figure (Nut) who is protectively bent over the Earth, enveloping it and them serenely' (50).

I would suggest that what is blocking Bettelheim from appreciating the full power of at least the best of the stories has much to do with this understanding of the way they use images. In order to understand the meaning of a symbol, at least as Bettelheim uses that term, all we need to do is appreciate what object or event it is meant to refer to—to designate. Thus, he is satisfied as to the symbolic meaning of a wolf when he concludes that it *refers to* a seducer. He is satisfied that he appreciates the meaning of the figure of mother when he realizes that it is a way to *designate* the heavens and sky. But, if we are satisfied that we fully appreciate what an image can accomplish once we think we know what object or event it is attempting to designate, we actually close ourselves off from the possibility that at least the best images can do more than just *refer* to a thing or event. As we saw with Dante and as we see again here, they can also help us to understand something of the nature of the thing or event and even help us to judge it. They can do so when they manage not just to refer to a thing but also to indicate what it is *like*. Images that manage to do this qualify as metaphors by doing something quite different from what symbols do.

So far we are attributing Bettelheim's blindness to the metaphoric quality of fairy tales both to his orthodox Freudianism and his underlying assumption that the purpose of language, even in fiction, is merely to refer to objects rather than help us understand and evaluate them by portraying what they are like. But there is also an additional factor. We have said that fairy tales utilize a *specific* kind of metaphor. In the case of fairy tales, what things are claimed to be like are *magical* things. What, in Bettelheim's grasp of the function of images, might leave him with a particular aversion to *this* sort of metaphor?

As noted above, Bettelheim attributed the ancient Egyptians' image of the sky and heavens as a motherly figure to their pre-scientific level of understanding. However, instead of treating that as a bad thing, he offers a defense, albeit a heavily qualified one, of this image:

> Far from preventing man from later developing a more rational explanation of the world, such a view offers security which, when the time is ripe, allows for a truly rational world view […] To deprecate protective imagery like this as mere childish projections of an immature mind is to rob the young child of one aspect of the prolonged safety and comfort he needs. (Bettelheim 1991: 50)

Without necessarily assuming that the ancient Egyptians realized this, it can certainly be suggested that the image they invented can be formulated, not (as Bettelheim assumes) just as a pre-rational explanation of the world but as a potentially fitting metaphor for what at least a benign (Egyptian?) sky *is* like in its relation to the Earth. It *is* like a protective, motherly, enveloping figure. Bettelheim, then, might be conflating being able to find a rational explanation for a thing such as the sky with the need to therefore abandon (as childish, as pre-scientific) some types of metaphors.

In this light, it is worth examining a brief passage where it does seem that Bettelheim might be perceiving a fairy tale as metaphoric rather than symbolic. He writes:

> A child, for example, who has learned from fairy stories to believe that what at first seemed a repulsive, threatening figure can magically change into a most helpful friend is ready to

believe that a strange child whom he meets and fears may also be changed from a menace into a desirable companion. Belief in the 'truth' of the fairy tale gives him courage not to withdraw because of the way the stranger appears to him at first. Recalling how the hero of many a fairy tale succeeded in life because he dared to befriend a seemingly unpleasant figure, the child believes he may work the same magic. (Bettelheim 1991: 50)

Bettelheim is thinking of stories like 'Beauty and the Beast' in which a beast is magically changed into a handsome prince once Beauty comes to truly care for him. As distinct from when he offers his detailed analysis of this story later in the book, here Bettelheim eschews a Freudian interpretation. By discussing the kind of change that 'Beauty and the Beast' portrays in the same breath as the change that a child might experience in how a stranger can appear to him, Bettelheim does seem close to understanding that the story has invented a metaphor that helps to depict the nature of something that can happen in real life. But it is in keeping with his notion that children, like primitives, take things as literally true that he suggests that the child, in how s/he relates to a stranger, believes s/he can work *the same* magic.[4] According to Bettelheim, then, the image is not just a metaphor to the child.

But what is the image to Bettelheim? By suggesting that what actually produces the change from a threatening and, indeed, even repulsive figure to a most helpful friend is merely the fact that the child does not withdraw, Bettelheim clearly wants to display his understanding that the event is not really magical at all. Instead, it can easily be encompassed within 'a truly rational world view.' However, while we can agree that no magic needs to be posited here, that does not foreclose the concern that Bettelheim's confident way of explaining how this is totally different from magic, designed of course to contrast with the child's (and childish) view that it is actually the same as magic, could at the very least weaken his understanding that, while he is no doubt right that there is no magic here, yet, there really is something *like* magic—something wonderful—something enchanting—about such a complete and total transformation, particularly if it is produced by, as he says, someone doing nothing more active than just not withdrawing from the scene. Even if we agree with him that such an event does have a rational explanation,[5] that does not mean we need to abandon the use of metaphors, as a metaphor that suggests how magic-like an event is has a major role to play in conveying an important feature, i.e. the enchanting quality, of this particular event.

A major part of Bettelheim's defense of the best fairy tales is that they manage to teach children moral lessons. Other stories are much less effective in this regard:

Obviously, not every story contained in a collection called 'Fairy Tales' meets these criteria. Many of these stories are simply diversions, cautionary tales, or fables. If they are fables, they tell by means of words, actions, or events—fabulous though these may be—what one ought to do. (Bettelheim 1991: 27)

I would suggest that we could identify cautionary tales and fables by their lack of compelling metaphors, and this would be because they are too interested in directly telling children how the authors think they should behave. A good metaphor for something, say a housewife or an act of seduction, might be *implying* that something is bad but it would also have to be relaxed enough about the thing to want to portray it rather than merely condemn it. The theme of how metaphors and related ideas are of value in teaching (and not just teaching children) will be returned to in Chapter 9.

Another positive feature of the fairy tales that Bettelheim most admires is, according to him, that they are aesthetically satisfying:

> The delight we experience when we allow ourselves to respond to a fairy tale, the enchantment we feel, comes not from the psychological meaning of a tale (though that contributes to it) but from its literary qualities—the tale itself as a work of art. (Bettelheim 1991: 12)

Obviously what is glossed here are the notions of literary quality and, similarly, managing to be a work of art. Arguably, the ones that seem artful (and this is not all of them) are the same ones that manage illuminating metaphors. Whether and how metaphors are related to aesthetic quality will be a major theme of the next chapter and also the final chapter.

Suggesting, as has been done in this chapter, that the way to defend Bettelheim's core insight that fairy tales do illuminate reality is to understand their metaphoric quality is meant to serve a wider purpose. Even though nothing approximating a logically valid conclusion is reached in the stories we discussed, they do manage, as does Dante, a form of judgment. They display something of the nature of various possible actions, in the case of Little Red Riding Hood, the action of seduction, in the case of Snow White, the action of restricting oneself to domestic concerns, and in the case of Cinderella, the action of getting what one deserves in life.

Notes

1 See, for example, Belotti 1978.

2 The novelist Donald Barthelme's 1968 rendering of the story is an attempt to interpret Snow White's life with the dwarfs in the same way I am doing here.

3 For a similar critique of the notion of the symbol which also suggests that another version of Freud can enlist him in the critique, see Didi-Huberman 2005.

4 In terms of the distinctive senses of 'the same ' discussed in the Introduction, Bettelheim is using the work in Ricouer's rather than Heidegger's sense.

5 Of course, not even today have we managed to provide rational, if by that we mean scientific, explanations of all things that happen, particularly between persons.

Chapter 3

Sontag's Critique of Metaphors

W e began by suggesting that the standard way of arriving at judgments, by syllogisms, has not fulfilled its promise. The alternative, judging by making comparisons, comes to seem viable once it is appreciated that interpreting the identity of any phenomenon is, contrary to the assumption as to the nature of being that goes back to Aristotle and others, a matter of what differentiates that phenomenon. Metaphors therefore become potential tools for exercising judgments. What, in particular, metaphoric reasoning can accomplish began to be displayed in the last two chapters. Though metaphors undeniably remain in the realm of aesthetics, it is hoped that they no longer seem second best.

But now another, potentially even more damaging, criticism of our emerging method will be considered. There is at least one author who, in how one could analyze certain material, actually wants to *ban* metaphors. In a work such as this, aiming to defend metaphoric reasoning, it is surely relevant to engage with the well-known attack on metaphors launched by Susan Sontag. Highly critical both of the widespread use of metaphors to depict illnesses and, equally, the wide spread use of illness metaphors to depict other things, she writes: 'My point is that illness is not a metaphor, and that the most truthful way of regarding illness—and the healthiest way of being ill—is one most purified, most resistant to, metaphoric thinking' (Sontag 1977: 3).

What she most wants purified in this way are discussions of tuberculosis and cancer. She calls the metaphors associated with them 'fantasies' and claims their existence is temporary: 'The fantasies inspired by TB in the last century, by cancer now, are responses to a disease thought to be intractable and capricious—that is, a disease not understood [...] Such a disease is, by definition, mysterious' (Sontag 1977: 5).

Once the causes are known, the mystery will disappear, and so will the need for metaphors:

> For as long as its cause was not understood and the ministrations of doctors remained so ineffective, TB was thought to be an insidious, implacable theft of a life. Now it is cancer's turn to be the disease that doesn't knock before it enters, cancer that fills the role of an illness experienced as a ruthless, secret invasion—a role it will keep until, one day, its aetiology becomes as clear and its treatment as effective as those of TB have become. (Sontag 1977: 5)

The prediction that cancer metaphors will some day become unnecessary and so die out seems logical given two assumptions: (1) Cancer metaphors and TB metaphors are fantasies. (2) Disease fantasies arise when aetiology is unclear and disappear when aetiology is clear.

As such, there is an additional relevance for us of Sontag's way of arguing. Assumption 1 amounts to a minor premise. Assumption 2 amounts to a major premise, so, in order to arrive at the negative judgment of metaphors, she is using the very tool we insisted should be replaced by metaphors, namely a syllogism.

An issue to consider, then, is whether either her major or minor premise is any more factually sound than the ones considered in the Introduction. First, then, can it really be shown that there is a causal link between the presence and absence of disease fantasies and knowledge of a disease's aetiology? For example, does the assumption work for heart disease? Sontag writes: 'Cardiac disease implies a weakness, trouble, failure that is mechanical; there is not a disgrace, nothing of the taboo that once surrounded people afflicted with TB and still surrounds those who have cancer' (Sontag 1977: 9).

While, to her credit, she readily acknowledges the fact that there are no such fantasies about heart disease, it has to be said that this fact constitutes a major trouble for any straightforward version of Sontag's disease/fantasy connection. Since, like cancer, but unlike TB, heart disease *is* currently without either clear cause or definite cure, the straightforward application of Sontag's major premise would require that heart disease *should* have fantasies associated with it. While the passage suggests this case does not make Sontag think she must relinquish her assumption, it does require her to engage in the repair work of explaining away an exception. She tries to argue, in a move that strictly speaking involves her in utilizing what she avowedly wishes to resist, namely a current prejudice about a disease, that heart disease is 'mechanical,' and this accounts for why the fantasies that the supposed discovery of her law predicts have not materialized. Sontag's 'discovery' of a law already seems less convincing as it is only surviving with the help of interpretive work that attempts to neutralize an admittedly anomalous case.

While heart disease represents a difficult to justify exception as there are no cancer-like fantasies attached to it even though there is no clear cure, there are certainly other diseases besides TB and cancer that, when they lacked clear causes or cures, *did* generate fantasies. Sontag writes, no doubt accurately, about leprosy: 'Leprosy in its heyday arouses a […] disproportionate sense of horror. In the Middle Ages, the leper was a social text in which corruption was made visible, an exemplum, an emblem of decay' (Sontag 1977: 58).

Leprosy, she goes on to say, shows that 'any important disease whose causality is murky, and for which treatment is ineffectual, tends to be awash in significance' (Sontag 1977: 58). But, to treat leprosy as quite as clear a case of the supposed link as TB, Sontag has to ignore one aspect of the fantasies around leprosy. She depicts leprosy as a disease in whose 'heyday,' the Middle Ages, disproportionate horror was aroused but she fails to make anything of the fact, awkward for her claims, that unlike TB, it is hardly evident that the horror has now disappeared even though the cause and cure are better understood. Sontag's 'discovery' of a law survives only with the help of an interpretation of the current situation that ignores part of the full story of leprosy.

Furthermore, even in the two cases where Sontag's idea seems most convincing, what is problematic is that the fantasy effects do not work in the same way. While both TB and cancer have certainly attracted fantasies, the content of the respective fantasies reveals at least one substantial difference. With TB, the 'agony became romantic in a stylized account of the disease's preliminary symptoms (for example debility is transformed into languor) and the actual agony was suppressed' (Sontag 1977: 29). On the other hand, with cancer, all the fantasies not withstanding, it is 'a disease which nobody has managed to glamorize' (35).

The idea that cancer and TB fantasies can be explained by a single law becomes much less plausible once it is acknowledged that the fantasies appear to function so differently. Sontag responds to this awkward fact with yet more unconvincing repair work. She suggests that, even though cancer is not glamorized in our era, that does not necessarily imply what we could easily think, i.e. that our disease fantasies are so different in the two cases that no overall law can depict both of them. Instead:

> In the twentieth century the cluster of metaphors and attitudes formerly attached to TB split up and are parcelled out to two diseases. Some features of TB go to insanity: [...] someone too sensitive to bear the horrors of the vulgar, everyday world. Other features go to cancer—the agonies that can't be romanticized. (Sontag 1977: 36)

Here the blatant fudge is that Sontag is attempting to still maintain the validity of her major premise even though she admits that it only fully fits just *one* case. The existence of a contemporary supposed 'best case' that we now discover only half fits, does not, she expects us to believe, matter because she can point to another contemporary case that supplies the missing half.

If we can now safely conclude that her major premise is not confirmed, even by facts Sontag herself acknowledges, what of her minor premise that illness metaphors are nothing but fantasies? As a typical fantasy about TB, she cites an excerpt from one of Franz Kafka's letters:

> The diseases around which the modern fantasies have gathered—TB, cancer—are viewed as forms of self-judgement, of self-betrayal. One's mind betrays one's body. 'My head and lungs have come to an agreement without my knowledge,' Kafka said about his TB in a letter to Max Brod in September 1917. (Sontag 1977: 40)

Kafka, Sontag believes, is simply laboring under a delusion about the aetiology of his illness. She thinks he should recognize that just because his lungs are bleeding, that does not mean they have agreed to anything. That fact does not mean anything except that he has tuberculosis.

While thus far it could seem as if Kafka simply misunderstands an illness, that impression changes if we begin to consider a somewhat fuller version of his letter. Kafka wrote:

> I am constantly seeking an explanation for this disease, for I did not seek it. Sometimes it seems to me that my brain and lungs came to an agreement without my knowledge. 'Things can't go on this way,' said my brain, and after five years the lungs said they were ready to help. (Kafka 1978: 138)

The 'things' that he is referring to that happened after five years were his first haemorrhage and the decision he made immediately after it to end his long engagement to Felice Bauer.

At first, the fact that Kafka says he is seeking an explanation because he knows that he did not wish his disease on himself could make it seem that, as Sontag believes, he is simply unaware that diseases have natural causes. But then we learn that his attempts at an explanation are stimulated, not merely by the fact that he contracted the disease without wanting it, but by the fact that what the disease produced, i.e. the end of his engagement, was something he *was* thinking should happen. Kafka is saying that he would not have been so intent on an explanation if either of two facts had not been the case: if the disease that brought about the desirable outcome *had* been produced by his efforts or if the disease had not resulted in such a desirable result. He only wants an explanation because of the fact that a disease that he certainly made no effort whatsoever to produce had immediately managed to achieve just the outcome that, while he had been conscious it was the right one, he had been unable, for five full years, to achieve by his own efforts.

It is true that something like Sontag's view of Kafka's mistake could still be maintained even with this fuller view of the events, though now the mistake would be that what he does not realize is that coincidences can happen. But if Kafka could be convinced that the disease is just a coincidence, would that satisfy his need for an explanation? Why is it that even people who are not superstitious in our enlightened times who bump into an acquaintance they happen to be thinking about at the time tend to remark on it? Isn't it remarkable in the literal sense? It can be suggested that the reason for this is not, or at least not only, some vague belief in psychic powers. Instead, there is a strong element of wanting to set the record straight. 'Funny, I was just thinking about you,' helps to make it clear, certainly much clearer than it would otherwise be, that though what happened is an accident, it is not one you in any way wished to avoid. One is trying to explain but not in the sense of looking for a mysterious cause but in the sense of trying to interpret an event that it is particularly possible to interpret in another way.

Kafka can be read as trying to explain but in the sense of interpreting an event or, to be more precise, the relation between two events, his illness and the end of his engagement, events that could certainly, were it not for his efforts, be interpreted in quite another way. Given the bare facts, i.e. he was engaged but he broke it off when he became ill, if required to interpret this, we would be likely to conclude (wrongly) that Kafka had made up his mind to get married but then changed his mind when he got the disease. Kafka, I think we can now say, is not suffering from any illusion and so we can conclude that Sontag's idea that his resort to metaphoric reasoning is a mere fantasy seems mistaken. We can suggest, instead, that we are witnessing another instance of what we have seen in previous chapters. In particular the idea that what the decision to break off the engagement was *like* was an agreement between his brain and lungs without his knowledge, is a metaphor that helps us to interpret the nature of the decision as one that, while he was never able to actually make it, was at the same time not really one that went against his will.

Although it has been shown, both that metaphors cannot be equated with fantasies and that Sontag's prediction that cancer metaphors will disappear once the disease's aetiology is known cannot really be seen as logical, there is evidence that these demonstrations would not be enough to end her resistance to metaphoric thinking. Metaphors for illnesses, as we have just seen in the case of Kafka, are certainly part of an effort to interpret those illnesses and Sontag, it can be shown, believes that even when, as is currently the case with cancer, aetiology is unclear, that is simply the wrong response to illness. She writes: 'Nothing is more punitive than to give a disease a meaning' (Sontag 1977: 58). She objects whenever 'diseases and patients become subjects for decipherment' (45). In the same vein, one should never interpret a disease because a disease is 'just a disease' (7).

While, at first, it seems plausible to identify comments like these with Aristotle's pro-philosophy, anti-aesthetics stance, actually anyone familiar with Sontag's early work, written well before the book we are discussing, is likely to arrive at the opposite conclusion. In a famous early piece not at all about illness, we find Sontag expressing similar statements. For example: 'To interpret is to impoverish, to deplete the world—in order to set up a shadow world of "meanings"' (Sontag 1967a: 7). Or: 'Away with all duplicates […] until we again experience more immediately what we already have' (7). One should avoid at all costs attempts to 'show what it means' (14). But, since here Sontag was discussing the fallacy not of interpreting disease but of interpreting art, we can say that whereas Aristotle disparaged metaphors because of his conception of the limits of aesthetic reasoning, Sontag actually opposes metaphors *for* aesthetic reasons. Sontag once wrote: 'In place of a hermeneutics we need an erotics of art' (14). Though this formulation of her argument would not be welcomed by her, it seems that Sontag now wants an erotics of cancer.

In order to get a deeper understanding of Sontag's resistance to metaphor, it seems necessary to understand how her commitment to aesthetics could have helped form that resistance. In the earlier piece, Sontag resisted interpretation because:

Even in modern times, when most artists and critics have discarded the theory of art as representation of an outer reality in favour of art as subjective expression, the main feature of the mimetic theory persists. Whether we conceive of art on the model of a picture (art as a picture of reality) or on the model of a statement (art as the statement of the artist), content still comes first. The content may have changed. It may now be less figurative, less lucidly realistic. But it is still assumed that a work of art *is* its content. Or, as it is usually put today, that a work of art by definition says something. (Sontag 1967a: 4, original emphasis)

She means that, even though most now recognize that art need not picture reality, there is still a tendency to look for an external referent to which the art corresponds. For example, she objects that, for Freudians, to analyze a work of art is to translate, 'to restate the phenomenon, in effect to find an equivalent for it' (Sontag 1967a: 7). Bettelheim's search for symbolic meanings in fairy tales is a case in point. Sontag's warning about reducing art to its supposed content is important but some contemporary theorists are very much alive to this danger without accepting Sontag's conclusion that the only alternative is to think of art and one's comments on it as needing to be against interpretation. For example, Christophe Menke resists Sontag's 'flight from interpretation' and in particular her just-quoted slogan (Menke 1998: 15). Similarly, while Georges Didi-Huberman joins Sontag in denying that art either is a picture of reality—a view he traces to Vasari—or some code-like sign—the view of Panofsky—his alternative is not what Menke labels Sontag's 'crudely fashioned' one (15).

Though it could seem at first to take us away from our central topic, Didi-Huberman's way of understanding what art can do and, therefore, the place of interpretation, is worth considering in some detail. We shall look at his way of *aesthetically* appreciating—the approach Sontag bemoans the absence of in most interpretations—three paintings. First, approaching a fresco by Fra Angelico in the San Marco Monastery (circa 1438–45), he notes that there is a difficulty in even seeing the painting, much less what it is about. The painting has 'the initial effect of luminous obfuscation' (Didi-Huberman 2005: 11). This is because

> next to the fresco is a small window, facing east, that provides enough light to envelop our faces, to veil in advance the anticipated spectacle. Deliberately painted 'against' this light, Angelico's fresco obscures the obvious fact of its own presence. (Didi-Huberman 2005: 11)

Even when one does, eventually, manage to see the painting, the sensation of light obscuring the image remains:

> After one's eyes have adjusted to the light, this impression is oddly persistent: the fresco 'comes clear' only to revert to the white of the wall, for it consists only of two or three stains of attenuated colour placed against a slightly shaded background of the same whitewash. Thus where natural light besieged our gaze—and almost blinded us—there is henceforth white, the pigmentary white of the background, which comes to possess us. (Didi-Huberman 2005: 11)

Eventually, the figures in the fresco become clear enough so that we can realize we are seeing Fra Angelico's version of the Annunciation. However, in keeping with our initial impression it seems 'the most poorly and summarily recounted story there can be. No salient details [...] there's nothing picturesque in this painting; it's as taciturn as they come' (Didi-Huberman 2005: 14).

Didi-Huberman's challenge is to defend the painting and Fra Angelico against the charge that he has merely made a careless, even incompetent (because lacking 'realistic' detail) painting of a subject that others have done much better. What Didi-Huberman asks us to consider in order to defend the painting is the nature of its subject. In approaching the Annunciation we are, of course, approaching no ordinary event. Instead 'it is called the inconceivable, the *mystery*. It offers itself in the pulse of an ever singular, ever dazzling event: that obscure self-evidence that Saint Thomas here calls a revelation' (Didi-Huberman 2005: 211).

Didi-Huberman's idea is that what accounts for the otherwise hard to explain features—both what is there including even its placing with regard to the window, and what it lacks—the details—is that Fra Angelico is *not* trying to make the event 'visible' (Didi-Huberman 2005: 17). In fact, in this version, the Annunciation 'is not visible' (17). *That* accomplishment would have required a much clearer picture of Gabriel, Mary, Nazareth, etc. Instead he is trying to help us *visualize*—envision—the mysterious revelation that this event is. Instead of a picture that attempts to *correspond* to an event, we get a visual image that has the effect (intended and arguably achieved) of helping us to imagine the nature of the event. What is worthy of note for our purposes is Didi-Huberman's ability to see art as not a copy but still as managing to be an interpretation.

Didi-Huberman's version of art does not apply just to paintings as clearly unrealistic as this one nor to subjects as obviously mysterious as the Annunciation. Peter Breughel's painting of the Fall of Icarus (c. 1558) is famed for its apparently realistic details, in particular the fact that Breughel is careful to make the feathers that the sun has melted, causing Icarus to fall, not fall as quickly at Icarus himself. And, as Didi-Huberman points out, these feathers can also be seen, à la Panofsky, as 'an iconographic attribute necessary for the representation of the mythological scene' (Didi-Huberman 2005: 238). However, in studying the painting, he also notes a feature that violates the apparent realism: 'The details called "feathers" have no distinctive features that "separate" them completely from the foam produced, in the sea, by the falling body' (238).

While it is tempting to treat this fact as a flaw, in that feathers and foam, though both may be white, certainly do not have an identical appearance, Didi-Huberman suggests that the lack of differentiation between what is in the air and what is in the water produces 'a kind of figural vertigo, but a vertigo that effectively flattens the painting [...] the whole picture functions [...] like an extravagant bending of space' (Didi-Huberman 2005: 239).

He means that Breughel has done more than make the fall, in Didi-Huberman's terms, 'visible.' Like Fra Angelico helping us to envision the Annunciation, Breughel helps us envision—imagine—the act—the event—of falling, crashing even, into the sea.

Another artist noted for his apparent realism is Jan Vermeer. Didi-Huberman focuses on how some threads, threads certainly not being a self-evidently mysterious object like the Annunciation or even the Fall of Icarus, are painted in *The Lacemaker (c.1669–70)*: 'We recognize, almost without reflection, some red thread spilling out of a sewing basket' (Didi-Huberman 2005: 254).

But, looking at this detail carefully, what it consists of is something other than a realistic representation of threads. Instead 'a flow of red paint [...] gushes forth [...] It unravels madly [...] Its outline seems to wander; its very schema makes a stain' (Didi-Huberman 2005: 253–4).

Didi-Huberman cites another critic who sees 'thread that is poorly described, confused' (Alpers 1983: 31–2, quoted in Didi-Huberman 2005: 255). According to her, Vermeer is guilty of 'a flaw or failure, an accident of description' (Alpers 1983: 31–2, quoted in Didi-Huberman 2005: 255). But, even though threads are admittedly a mundane thing, not apparently worthy of much thought, what if Vermeer is not so much trying to describe them as helping us envision something of what they are like? Didi-Huberman's version of this aspiration is that it is 'as though Vermeer had been interested only in the process—in the unravelling, the flow' (Didi-Huberman 2005: 255). He has found a visual way to help us envision an aspect of thread, perhaps its unruly quality before the lacemaker has domesticated it, just as Fra Angelico helps us envision the mystery of a reported biblical event or Breughel what it would be like to fall into the ocean.

The view of art developed here has important implications both for how we think about art itself and art's relation to other things, including illness. If art does not have to be either representative or symbolic to be able to be, in some sense, about other things than itself, then we are relieved of Sontag's concern that art cannot be relevant to those things without sacrificing its nature as art. At the same time, that art can say something relevant about those things—the Annunciation, the Fall of Icarus, even thread—means that, contrary to Sontag, other things, even things whose causes are known, can still be clarified by the kind of decipherment art offers.

Furthermore, while it would be wrong to derive from Didi-Huberman's analysis of art the conclusion that all such interpretive art amounts to finding metaphors for things, it is at least suggestive that, in trying to articulate the status of Vermeer's red flow of paint, he writes: 'It is perhaps "thread-like" but it is not painted like thread' (Didi-Huberman 2005: 255).

If it were painted like thread the red would be an attempt to copy thread, but by being thread-like we can perhaps say that the way it helps to reveal thread, in particular its quality of unraveling, is by finding something that it seems appropriate to *compare* thread to. It works, then, like a metaphor, revealing something of the nature of thread by finding something to which it is similar.

That aesthetic reasoning, including metaphors, could clarify disease can now be seen to imply that, contrary to Sontag, diseases are *not* just diseases if by that it means there is nothing left to interpret or judge about them. A recent work by Alan Blum is relevant because it would suggest that Sontag's approach has the consequence of ceding all authority to the medical model of disease. Reflecting, in particular, on the movement to redefine obesity as a disease, without himself denying that there could be 'somatic causes', Blum suggests that

> when any condition such as obesity is conceded to be a disease, this is tantamount to passing its interpretive control to medicine and to giving medicine the right to treat the condition technically. While these implications are not fully understood, they do suggest that it is the fate of obesity to be formulated technically according to conditions that always risk preserving its weakness, as if the effort to survive it at any cost is the strongest relation imaginable. (Blum 2011: 175)

We can say that, by contrast, Kafka's metaphor is one attempt to have a stronger relationship to disease by refusing to let it be only a medical condition and to do so by trying to articulate a way in which he need not exactly disavow its place as part of his 'intimate history' (Blum 2011: 175) even if he rids himself of any unscientific fantasies about it. Or, an even more obvious example, Sontag's would-be ban on metaphors becomes particularly hard to credit in her analysis of the response to cancer of the novelist Alice James: 'Alice James, writing in her journal a year before she died from cancer in 1892, speaks of "the unholy granite substance in my breast"' (Sontag 1977: 13).

Sontag expects us to treat this as a misinterpretation of a tumor when it is surely better seen as James at the very least supplementing medical determinations and showing her continuing strength as a writer by coming up with an illuminating metaphor for what she is going through.

In so doing, it can be noted that she also provides a solution of sorts to the perennial philosophical problem of whether we can know another's pain. Ludwig Wittgenstein who, of course, has argued that we can, also makes the point that accomplishing the task can be none too easy:

> If one has to imagine someone else's pain on the model of one's own, this is none too easy a thing to do: for I have to imagine pain which I do *not feel* on the model of the pain which I *do feel*. (Wittgenstein 1958: 101, original emphasis)

Wittgenstein does not actually indicate what we need to do to make pain not private. What James does, hints at how this problem could be solved. An apt metaphor such as James's can give others a kind of access to another's pain. Another example would be when a friend of mine described his arthritis as having to live with a terrorist. In dealing with this particular feature that Sontag obviously recognizes is present in many illnesses: the sheer pain associated with them, it seems especially perverse to object to the use of metaphors.

Our detour into Didi-Huberman's aesthetics has led to the conclusion that not just illness but other things as well could be illuminated by aesthetic reasoning. This returns us to the perspective of both Blum and McHugh and Derrida, cited in the Introduction and, hopefully, displayed in earlier chapters; a view that McHugh has more recently explicitly tied to the need for metaphors. He writes that identifying *anything* has the 'need, and a sustaining one, for the genesis of metaphor and simile' (McHugh 2008: 4).[1] He gives the example of how we manage to interpret 'the shout of "stop!" while observing a running figure with purse' as a robbery (4). What is critical to making the interpretation is working out what the shout and running are *like* and *unlike*. In particular it helps to see—to interpret—what this specific shout means to notice that it is *not* like a murmur, and to interpret what this running means to see that it is *not* like jogging:

> It is in the simultaneous work on the possible difference or not of the possible identities of each that is iterated or completed in generating robbery as the signified, work which cannot be stipulated in advance or according to rule. (McHugh 2008: 3)

Still further support for this view of meaning formation can be found, within philosophy, in the theory of identity formation associated with Saul Kripke. Kripke shows that the way we manage to identify objects, except for ones whose identity is given by their proper names, is by determining whether they have some essential properties. In turn, the way we identify what these essential properties are is by imagining what properties would make them so *unlike* themselves as to be a completely different thing. For example in speaking of ex-President Nixon: even if 'we suppose Nixon to have done different things, we assume we are still talking about Nixon himself' (Kripke 1977: 83). On the other hand, there are properties of an object: 'such that if an object did not have it, it would not be this object' (86). In McHugh's terms, if a noise were like a murmur, that would not help us to interpret it as a different sort of shout (like some hypothetical different sort of Nixon who joined a radical student group). Instead that sort of difference would make it something other than a shout.

In contrast with this emerging view that we need metaphoric thinking to manage to identify anything, Sontag, as we said, extends her critique of illness metaphors to those who use illness as a metaphor to depict other things:

> Trying to comprehend 'radical' or 'absolute' evil, we search for adequate metaphors. But the modern disease metaphors are all cheap shots. The people who have the real disease are also hardly helped by hearing their disease's name constantly being dropped as the epitome of evil. Only in the most limited sense is any historical event or problem like an illness. (Sontag 1977: 85)

The sense in which *no* events are exactly like illnesses would perhaps be that none amounts to a condition of an individual. But, as exactitude is not really a requirement or for that matter a possibility for even the best metaphor, metaphors not being, as we have hopefully made clear throughout, either copies of anything or identical to what they resemble, she must have other grounds for such a ban. The passage just cited does suggest another objection to illness metaphors: it is wrong to use them to depict how absolutely evil a thing is. Her specific complaint about metaphors in the case that most concerns her is that 'the use of cancer as a metaphor [...] amounts to saying, first of all, that the event or situation is unqualifiedly or unredeemably wicked' (Sontag 1977: 83).

While this does seem a stronger argument against the use of illness metaphors than just that they are not identical to an illness, not least because, as Sontag points out, they could seem to be belittling real disease victims by suggesting their disease is like something evil, it does raise the question of whether her analysis of this way of deploying metaphors is accurate. In particular, while we should agree that if anything really is absolutely evil—as that would seem to remove any room for ambiguity as to its identity—metaphors might well not be required, is this really what metaphors, even cancer metaphors, are doing?[2]

One of her examples is a metaphor that she, famously, once used and now regrets: 'I once wrote, in the heat of despair over America's war on Vietnam, that "the white race is the cancer of human history"' (Sontag 1977: 85). We know from her self-criticism that she thinks she is here making the mistake of using an illness metaphor in order to help convey how absolutely evil something is, but it is actually unclear what she thinks is absolutely evil, the white race or the war in Vietnam. Probably because she is now ashamed of what she wrote, Sontag does not quote it in full but, as with the Kafka case, doing so may move our analysis along. What she actually wrote was:

> The truth is that Mozart, Pascal, Boolean algebra, Shakespeare, parliamentary government, baroque churches, Newton, the emancipation of women, Kant, Marx, Balanchine ballet et al. don't redeem what this particular civilization has wrought upon the world. The white race is the cancer of human history. It is the white race and it alone—its ideologies and inventions—which eradicates autonomous civilizations whenever it spreads, which has upset the ecological balance of the planet, which now threatens the very existence of life itself. (Sontag 1967b: 57–58)

Even as this passage makes it slightly clearer how Sontag could have felt comfortable offering her metaphor, i.e. she does actually try for resemblances such as that both cancer and the white race spread things that are destructive, the main point we can extract is that, whatever she was trying to understand as absolutely evil—unqualifiedly wicked—it cannot have been the white race since she notes so many good things about it. Nothing can be absolutely evil if it has produced so much good. It must therefore have been the Vietnam War that Sontag was feeling was unqualifiedly evil.

Considering the earlier passage in the light of her later explanation plus her more general comments about what is wrong with illness metaphors, it is possible to reconstruct the process by which Sontag arrived at her metaphor. Convinced that the Vietnam War was unqualifiedly wicked, she tried to think of the worst possible ('epitome of evil') epithet she could apply to its perpetrators. That they are like a cancer seemed sufficiently insulting. Any actual resemblance between what the perpetrators were doing and what cancer does, e.g. that both are spreading something, was secondary as she now concedes by *herself* omitting the portion of the passage that gives the metaphor whatever resonance it had.

Now, while it can be agreed that, as Sontag herself acknowledges, something has gone wrong in this case of metaphor selection, it can be suggested that the source of the problem is not the sheer fact that Sontag sought to compare a historical event to an illness. We have already said many times that metaphors are devices that can be used to help one interpret and judge events that one recognizes have ambiguities. This raises the question of what becomes of metaphors when one does *not* recognize any ambiguities in an event. If one recognizes no interpretive problem, then one would feel no need to help identify a thing by locating its similarities and differences from other and more familiar things. In the case of events that one felt were devoid of any ambiguity because of how clearly in the sense of absolutely evil they were, were one to use a negative metaphor at all, it might just be used for the purpose Sontag assumes it always has, i.e. just to epitomize (rather than interpret or judge) the evil of an event.

It follows that the real problem is not *any* attempt to use illness metaphors to interpret historical events but using metaphors, including illness metaphors, when one is not actually seeing the need for them because one does not recognize any ambiguities—any interpretive problem—in an event. It is therefore surely possible for some illness metaphors to be appropriate after all, namely ones when an author is actually using them to help him or her arrive at an interpretation of an event experienced, not as obviously evil, but as ambiguous. Sontag's would-be purge extends to the case when 'John Dean explained Watergate to Nixon: "we have a cancer within—close to the Presidency—that's growing"' (Sontag 1977: 84).

Sontag believes that Dean's mistake is the same as hers but, unlike hers, his metaphor *does* seem to be needed precisely because of ambiguities he is detecting in the event. Watergate appeared or could have appeared to be a small incident that could be safely ignored. The cancer metaphor manages, then, not merely to indicate that Dean thought Watergate was bad but to clarify precisely what could otherwise be quite ambiguous about it, that as trivial as it could appear and as tempting as it could therefore be to ignore it, it was not likely to go away, was likely to become more of a problem for the president, and, if not dealt with, even had the capacity to prove fatal to him (as, of course, it was). This example makes it evident that it is not necessary to exclude all illness metaphors, only ones that do little or nothing to interpret ambiguous phenomena, which incidentally, could, assuming there is no clearly absolute evil (or good), be *all* phenomena.

So far this chapter has been assessing Sontag's arguments against metaphors. What remains to be demonstrated is perhaps even more telling: Sontag's main idea can be interpreted as *taking the form of a metaphor.* It is evident from the book as a whole that, while she thinks of herself as discovering an overall causal connection, her overriding interest is in the relation between two cases at two times, 19th-century TB and contemporary cancer. Given that we have seen both that no other cases really sit comfortably with the supposed causal law (or the syllogism implied by it) and that even the two cases she is particularly interested in do not seem fully subsumable under the law, it is worth considering whether Sontag's own results are more accurately viewed in some other way. There is an alternative way of perceiving her main point that does put her discoveries on a sounder footing but at the cost of casting some doubt on the viability of major implications of her work. That no other diseases are at all as clearly relevant to her anti-metaphor thesis as cancer and TB, and that even these two have significant differences between them, would no longer be such a problem if Sontag were seen as producing not a law but another case of what we have already seen both Dante and some authors of fairy tales producing, namely a very stimulating comparison. No other diseases need to fit and cancer does not have to work exactly like TB if what Sontag is doing is utilizing these cases not to argue for a general proposition but to help develop, via a comparison, an identity for cancer. Sontag's attempts to show what her reported facts actually signify, work much better when seen as this work of developing one disease's distinctive identity or meaning through a comparison with another thing, in relation to which it has both similarities and significant differences.

Thus, we already quoted her to the effect that while both cancer and TB have fantasies attached to them, the ones attached to cancer are 'far more punishing' (Sontag 1977: 47).

This is because there were 'glamour' and 'romantic values' attached to TB fantasies and 'mostly shame' attached to cancer (48). Putting aside grandiose claims to have uncovered some eternal law of the disease–fantasy relation, this and similar passages can be interpreted as suggesting a worthwhile idea: The myths surrounding cancer are such that one can say that to be a contemporary cancer sufferer is to be suffering a similar fate to a 19th-century TB sufferer but, alas, without any of the romance or glamour. While it is hard to deny that there is much that is illuminating about interpreting the fate of contemporary cancer victims in this way, it highlights the everyday and unnecessary cruelties that so many are subjected to because of (as Sontag rightly points out) preposterous prejudices. However, if her point is interpreted in this way, it is also hard to deny that, as her method involves depicting something (cancer) by depicting how something else (TB) is *like* it and *unlike* it, Sontag is dependent on the method of metaphor for her most stimulating observation.

However, any careful reading of her book would have to note that a great deal of what she appears to be trying to say is lost if Sontag's main point is interpreted as we have just done. In particular, the idea that illness cannot be a metaphor and the general injunction to avoid metaphoric thinking both would need to be abandoned.

So have we simply produced an interpretation that violates Sontag's intentions?

Ten years after writing the book we have been discussing, Sontag declares: 'Rereading *Illness as Metaphor* now, I thought: [...] Of course, one cannot think without metaphors. But that does not mean there aren't some metaphors we might well abstain from or try to retire' (Sontag 1988: 4–5).

Whether we interpret this as a revision of her views or (as she believes) only a clarification of what she meant, it is clear that Sontag herself, with hindsight, wishes she had not claimed that no metaphor could ever help depict an illness, or that no illness metaphor should ever be used to depict an event. She also explains what she *was* trying to say, both the target of her book and her purpose in writing it:

Twelve years ago, when I became a cancer patient, what particularly enraged me—and distracted me from my own terror and despair at my doctors' gloomy prognosis—was seeing how much the very reputation of this illness added to the suffering of those who have it [...] Many fellow patients [...] evinced disgust at their disease and a kind of shame. They seemed to be in the grip of fantasies about their illness by which I was quite unseduced. And it occurred to me that some of these notions were the converse of now thoroughly discredited beliefs about tuberculosis. As tuberculosis had often been regarded sentimentally, as an enhancement of identity, cancer was regarded with irrational revulsion, as a diminution of the self. (Sontag 1988: 12)

Two things can be noticed here. First, if *this* is what Sontag was trying to get across—to say—she actually did not express it well. By attempting to turn her perceptions and concerns into the discovery of a general law and a set of universal recommendations, all she managed to do was to mislead us as to her main points—what she actually meant to say. Second, at least arguably, the TB-cancer metaphor *does* express what we can now see her points—her message—to be. Her rage is on show—expressed—in her pointing to a resemblance between attitudes to cancer and a set of attitudes that we all know are nothing but preposterous fantasies. Her own terror and despair are successfully conveyed by comparing what it must be like to have her disease with having one that, in spite of all its agonies, at least offered the consolation of being accompanied by a soothing myth. At the same time, conviction as to the relevance of the comparison, would achieve her additional goal: Some distraction from the terror and despair by replacing them with their opposites, the courage and hope that follow from a further implication of the comparison, namely that we need put no more stock in the cancer fantasies, including their fatalistic content, than we would now put in TB fantasies.

So, if Sontag were to have put her insights forward as a way of interpreting what it means, what it is *like* to have cancer compared to what it was like to have had TB, beneficial outcomes would have followed. First, she would have stopped deceiving herself that she had managed to discover a general truth with concomitant general recommendations, thereby failing to notice how much fudging she was needing to do to bring recalcitrant material into line. Second, it even seems she would have found a much more suitable way to express what she later tells us she was meaning to say all along.

It is worth noting that this problem of making an apparent truth claim that she later tells us does not express her meaning is something that Sontag, throughout her career, was prone to. The notorious claim to have discovered the 'truth' about the white race can be seen as another example. We know that she later tells us that what she really meant to express was despair about America's behavior in Vietnam. She also adds that she was wishing to 'register indignation' (Sontag 1977: 85). If this is what she was feeling and meant to express, it is quite clear that, in spite of what she says, her feeling and purpose have not led her to a general truth. She could, then, have much more clearly expressed her meaning if she had exploited her despair and her desire to register indignation to help herself arrive, not at 'the' truth, but at some metaphor that could express the indignation as to what America had come to resemble such that not just Sontag but many people had, at least temporarily, come to despair at its behavior.

The overall conclusion of this chapter must be that Sontag's critique of metaphor fails in both prongs of her attack. It is both the case that metaphors can help us understand illnesses and that illness metaphors can be helpful in illuminating other aspects of reality.

Notes

1 It should be noted that his paper is really a supplement to an earlier work (McHugh 2007) and cannot properly be understood in isolation from this earlier paper.
2 In that he sees grades of evil, and the need for different metaphors to describe different types of it, even Dante does not see evil as an absolute.

Chapter 4[1]

Abortion

Having resisted a major attack on the whole idea of using metaphors, we return to considering how they can be productively employed. We have been arguing that the key to judging well is to work out the identity of the phenomenon that is being judged. One can do so by discovering what other things the phenomenon is like and unlike. Whereas we have thus far dismissed the claims of syllogisms to be effective forms of judgment, it can now be suggested that, once one accepts that the syllogisms used for judging contain not facts but plausible opinions, they can become useful after all. What they can provide are starting points in one's attempts to develop what is and what is not different about any phenomenon one wishes to judge. In this chapter and the next, we will further consider the syllogisms mentioned in the Introduction, not to prove anything, but to try to use material in them to help in arriving at defensible judgments about the admittedly controversial issues with which they are concerned. The material in these two chapters is drawn not from literary sources but from ongoing public and normally acrimonious debates.

We begin with a fuller statement of the typical syllogism, according to Macintyre, of those opposed to abortion:

> Murder is wrong. Murder is the taking of innocent life. An embryo is an identifiable individual, differing from a newborn infant only in being at an earlier stage on the long road to adult capacities and, if any life is innocent, that of an embryo is. If infanticide is murder, as it is, abortion is murder. So abortion is not only morally wrong, but ought to be legally prohibited. (Macintyre 1985: 7)

While it cannot be accepted that there is anything here that qualifies as a definite fact, what is worth noting is that the passage does, for its cogency, depend on first recognizing and then dismissing the significance of an apparent difference. It is implicitly being conceded that an embryo appears *different* from an infant, by being at 'an earlier stage.' But then this difference is treated as not making a difference because both embryo and infant are on the same 'road.' While it is hard to believe that this difference will be as irrelevant as the passage (and those firmly against abortion) insists, it can be admitted that if this is the only difference between an embryo and an identifiable individual, abortions are more similar to murders than we might prefer to think and the act of abortion becomes at least somewhat more unsettling than it would otherwise be.

Sandel is another theorist who agrees that, without this difference being maintained, it is going to be more difficult to defend abortion. He writes that proponents of abortion must show 'that there is a relevant moral difference between aborting a foetus at a relatively early stage of development and killing a child' (Sandel 1996: 21).

Later we will suggest that, as it certainly is possible to work out moral differences that do depend on when the act is done and so between aborting a foetus and killing a child, it is misleading to conclude that abortions are that much *like* killing a child. However, is even the idea that, if there is no significant difference in these two acts, abortion is definitely and always wrong quite so self-evident? Sandel, somewhat surprisingly, is more ambivalent on this issue than Macintyre seems to be. While recognizing that not maintaining this difference makes it much harder to defend abortions, he actually denies it makes it exactly impossible. His argument is of particular relevance to us because it involves him in inventing a metaphor. He writes that, if abortions are like killing children, the only way to defend them is as 'an instance of just war theory,' but a just war in which there is 'the cost of some 1.5 million civilian deaths each year' (Sandel 1996: 21).

Even if abortion *is* like murder, then, it is a bit premature to assume, as does Macintyre's syllogism, that it must be wrong because, after all, there is at least one case in which something like murder is not necessarily wrong. This is the case of those who are killed in a just war. However, as Sandel immediately notes, there is a serious problem with using this comparison as a defense of abortion. In a just war, the form of killing that is most defensible is, of course, the deaths of fellow soldiers. Foetuses, Sandel says, are surely best seen as not like enemy soldiers but like the civilians, i.e. the non-combatants, that even the most just wars cannot totally eliminate the deaths of. As such, Sandel goes on to develop how, on reflection, his own metaphor does *not* seem to offer a credible defense of abortion. The trouble is that *this* 'war' cannot plausibly be seen as just, because it results in so many 'civilian casualties.' The huge number of 'casualties,' i.e. aborted embryos, that legalized abortion in fact results in, then, convinces Sandel that his metaphor does not, in the end, work to rescue abortion from the charge that it is unjust. But here he overlooks the fact that according to *his own* reasoning, it is the sheer *number* of deaths that is the problem. Even very just wars, unfortunately, will have *some* civilian casualties. Thus, if there could be substantially fewer casualties, at least *this* argument against abortion would be much less convincing. Such a reduction is perfectly possible. For example, were society to restrict abortion to cases where women had no access to contraception, obviously the number of abortions (at least legal ones) would go way down and then Sandel, for one, even if he continued to concede some resemblance between abortion and murder, could not so easily object to it.

We might say that, in some cases, the most obvious one being pregnancies caused by rape, what abortion seems most *like* is a form of birth control that, unfortunately, is the only one that is possible. In such cases, it should really be only those so extreme that they think even contraception is somehow like killing a child that would be opposed to it. It seems clear that, in cases like this, abortion is much easier to defend than in the case of a couple in a fully equal relationship who, knowing what could happen and with access to birth control, went ahead and had unprotected sex anyway. Here we see one clear value of the method of comparison. It allows us to see differences among abortions. Even if all abortions are like murdering someone, that does not mean that all abortions are alike.

In fact it is this, hardest to defend, form of abortion that is the main subject matter of this chapter. If it is at all plausible to agree with Sandel that abortion is a form of murder is it possible to defend *this* sort of abortion? If we are not to conclude that all such abortions are immoral, we are going to need to find some way to defend even this sort of abortion. To begin to do so, we will propose at least entertaining some uncomfortable ideas. We will suggest abandoning the idea that abortions are exactly just and even that they are particularly good. We will even need to consider whether there might be a form of murder that, if certainly not good, is at least among the least evil forms of murder we can imagine. In what follows, we will continue to attempt to judge abortion using the method of comparison.

As a way to begin on this, it is helpful to contemplate a case where someone, while not a murderer, does commit a major crime and yet never quite loses our sympathy. What is arguably the Coen brothers' best film, *Fargo (Joel Coen 1996)*, presents the case of a desperate man, Jerry Lundegaard. He has got himself into severe financial trouble and, while there is an obvious person who could bail him out, his father-in-law, this potential benefactor has no time for Jerry. Jerry is visibly desperate and comes up with a scheme where he hires two people to kidnap his wife in the hope that his father-in-law will pay the ransom. He intends to pay the kidnappers an agreed upon sum and use the balance to sort out his financial problems.

We cannot seriously argue that this kidnapping is not a crime. Jerry is therefore a criminal. Yet it does not seem right to label him all that evil. Many, myself included, even find him a sympathetic character. One aspect of the grounds for the sympathy is that, even though Jerry finds himself in a situation, financial trouble, that he presumably created, this seems an understandable mistake, something that could easily happen to the best of us. The consequences of the mistake are also not hard to relate to. Jerry is in a complete mess. Also, it really seems impossible to find a fully satisfactory way out because the only legal way out of it, asking his well to do father-in-law for the money, will not work. He is keeping our sympathy, then, because as unadmirable as the fake kidnapping is, it does seem the only way out of a terrible mess that he created by an understandable mistake. And a further factor is that, unlike many criminals, while it is undeniable that Jerry's actions result in some harm, not least to his wife, she being an innocent victim in all this, Jerry is the farthest thing from vicious. More than reluctant, he loathes the idea of causing anyone harm, as is demonstrated by the fact that he actually tries his best to call off the kidnapping when, for a time, it seems that another way out of the mess does become possible. Perhaps it could even be said that all this haplessness means that Jerry earns our affection as well as our sympathy. And, finally, though it would be absurd to say that anyone who would arrange to get his own wife kidnapped is admirable, there is even something that can be admired about Jerry. This would be the fact that he does try to do something about his situation. He tries to take his fate, such as it is, in his own hands rather than merely suffer. There is a kind of decisiveness that shows some strength of will, although the will on show is not in the service of anything higher than self-protection.

The similarities between what Jerry does and what some people contemplating an abortion might be facing are that both have made what could be an understandable mistake leading to a perceived terrible mess with no more palatable way out. As such, if they go through with it, they could well be said, if not to have justice on their side, to at least deserve our sympathy and even perhaps some sneaking admiration (for taking their fate in their own hands). However, there are at least two obstacles to accepting the comparison and therefore developing some empathy for this form of abortion. First, to what extent does the fact that Jerry comes off so lightly in our judgment of him stem from the fact that, because it is all a movie, he does not actually *do* anything? After all, some movies, e.g. *Bonnie and Clyde*, *Thelma and Louise (Arthur Penn 1967 Ridley Scott 1991)*, have managed sympathetic treatments even of serial killers. Even more to the point, Jerry *isn't* a killer, just a kidnapper, and in our efforts to face squarely the possible insights of anti-abortionists, we have conceded that that is precisely what anyone opting for an abortion can be seen as.

For there to be a better analogy, we would need to find, not another Hollywood movie, but a real-life murder that is both quite like some abortions and that somehow retains our sympathy. Worth thinking about in this vein is a political scandal that rocked 1970s Britain. In an era when homosexuality was still illegal, the then leader of the Liberal Party, Jeremy Thorpe, was being outed by one Norman Scott who claimed to have had an affair with him. According to agreed upon facts, one day a stranger bundled Scott and his dog into a car, took them to an isolated place, and shot the dog. According to Scott, the only reason the assassin did not also shoot him was because the gun jammed. In the subsequent trial, Scott accused Thorpe of hiring a hit man to murder him. In spite of considerable circumstantial events suggesting that Scott may well have got the facts right, Thorpe was not convicted.

It is a fact that, even when it was assumed that Thorpe did indeed attempt murder, many observers, myself included, felt that, even if we would be inclined to abandon the idea that he would make a particularly good prime minister, Thorpe's actions deserved some sympathy. If this story does, indeed, engage our sympathy and, among some, even a sneaking admiration, it does suggest that it is not so much the fact that Jerry in reality did not hurt anyone or even that he stopped short of murder that can account for our sympathetic reaction to him. Thorpe cannot fall back on either of these defenses but what he certainly does share with Jerry are other factors. He too has made an understandable mistake, in his case the alleged affair with someone willing to kiss and tell; a resultant terrible mess has ensued, in his case that his very promising career would be in tatters; and, finally, there is the lack of any more palatable way out, in his case the murder being the only feasible way to avoid having the consequences of his mistake hanging over him and perhaps spoiling the rest of his life.

And while there is the undeniable difference between the two cases that Thorpe, if he attempted murder, cannot plausibly be said to be trying his best not to harm Scott, it is surely the case that he is only seeking the most feasible way to remove him from the scene.

There is no active desire, unlike in many other forms of murder, to harm the victim. In this sense, the case actually has similarities with a more famous political scandal. While President Clinton did not attempt to murder Monica Lewinsky, he certainly did, as part of his efforts to extricate himself from *that* mess, instruct an aid to find her a job somewhere far away from him. Like Thorpe, he wanted to get rid of someone.

If these comparisons are sufficiently apt, what do they reveal? Abortions that follow this pattern are nothing to be proud of but to insist, with some justification, that they are a form of murder is not necessarily to have managed, contrary to the assumptions of the pro-life movement, quite so clear-cut a denunciation of them. Even if it seems a strange tack to take, what still needs to be addressed is whether we can imagine forms of murder that, while not particularly good, are not exactly evil either. What we have arrived at as at least defensible are ones that are the result of an understandable mistake that leads to a terrible mess where abortion seems the only feasible way out.

While I have suggested that this could be a way of defending some abortions, the same criteria can be used to judge as *less* defensible any abortions that can't be compared to what Jerry and Thorpe (if Scott is to be believed) did. If accepting that abortion is murder, we should also accept that if the pregnancy is *not* an understandable mistake or, even if it is, if the result *cannot* credibly be seen as a terrible mess or, even if it can be, if there is clearly a more palatable way out, the reasoning offered here would compel us to judge the decision less sympathetically. The argument, here, therefore, does not itself offer a defense for anyone for whom the pregnancy cannot plausibly be seen as an accident, or even for anyone for whom the pregnancy would be more accurately described as, while unplanned, more like an inconvenience rather than an outright mess, or even anyone who can envision a more palatable way out of what may well be something of a mess. In all these cases, besides the strongest defense that the sex was coerced or that all reasonable available precautions were taken, our additional defense will not work either.

Though our argument so far has been dependent on the sympathy it seems right to feel for Jeremy Thorpe being comparable to the sympathy we should feel for some kinds of abortions, there is a serious problem with taking the comparison too far. Even though it is undeniable that Thorpe bears some responsibility for the mess he is in, it may well be that some of our sympathy for him stems from our attitude toward his victim. Scott is not exactly blameless in that it was certainly in his power to avoid making life so difficult for Thorpe.[2] Obviously, foetuses have no such power, which is another way of saying that we cannot avoid seeing them as like the civilian casualties in a war.

But if part of our inclination to let Thorpe off the hook stems from the fact that his victim is not blameless, it should also be noted, that as with Jerry, our feelings about this case are bound to be mixed because even if his behavior is understandable, no one can seriously deny that what Thorpe might have been attempting deserves to be called a crime. As not just many people but many States are not prepared to take seriously the notion that abortion is a crime, surely that must be a mitigating factor in how harshly we judge the people who commit it. On the one hand, this conclusion must be right. On the other hand, it does raise an issue we have not yet considered: we know that many countries have legalized abortion but are they right to do so?

In beginning to discuss this and still using the method of comparison, we face a repeat of the situation faced earlier. Just as it becomes much harder to argue that it can be anything other than evil to have the kind of abortion we analyzed if one thinks abortion is like murder, it is equally hard to imagine how the State can legalize it if it is like the murder of an innocent. After all, most civilized States are hesitant to legalize *any* sort of murder, even capital punishment, much less the murders of those no one can argue have done anything wrong. Thus, as Sandel has shown, all known defenses of legalized abortion tend to presuppose that killing a foetus is *not* like murder (Sandel 1996: 100–3).

We begin what will inevitably be another uncomfortable discussion by wondering if the State has, wisely, legalized anything else that is sufficiently like what it is deciding to legalize when it legalized abortion. As a start, consider when the United States in 1933, decided that it was fighting a losing battle in banning alcohol and decided to end Prohibition. Like abortion, part of the decision was because people were doing it anyway. Yet, surely a large part of the willingness to legalize alcohol stems from a fact that would seem to most clearly *differentiate* it from abortion. Drinking of course has its victims but, by and large, the victim is the drinker himself whereas the main objection we have developed to abortion is that it results in blameless victims.

Recall, though, the main features of the type of abortion we found it both challenging and possible to defend. An understandable mistake leads to an accidental outcome that was unwanted, leading, if an abortion happens, to an innocent victim. What is worth reflecting on is that something like this *does* sometimes happen as a result of alcohol. Driving while drunk is *like* having unprotected sex in that even though we know it can lead to an unwanted accident, some of us sometimes do it anyway.

In that the State realizes that it cannot ban drinking, it does at first seem that it is powerless to prevent the inevitable accidents and victims that are going to result. However, relatively recently, some States have found a practical and, I would say, imaginative way that they can intervene. They impose a limit, i.e. on the amount that one can drink before one can drive, and that can help stop these unwanted accidents from happening.

But, in that there is no practical and even, perhaps, desirable way for States to regulate unprotected sex in the way some of them have started to regulate drink driving, it does seem an inevitable fact that, in this case, accidents will never stop happening. That is to say, unlike in the driving case, there is no feasible way to stop this sort of accident before it happens. But might this fact generate, not inertia, but an incentive to work out if there could be any other way of responding to this problem? If the result is truly unwanted and if there is no way to prevent it *before* it happens, might there not be an argument to try to give the person or persons best placed to decide whether they do want the outcome a *limited* opportunity to prevent, not the causes of the accident, that being no longer possible, but at least the effects of it? Instead of stopping an accident before it happens, we at least stop it as soon as possible after it happens.

This does not avoid innocent victims. That result would be an inevitable consequence of an unpreventable and unwanted accident that the person or persons responsible are unwilling to deal with in any other way. The result would be an abortion in the dictionary sense of the word. Something is cut short, here someone's life, but what could still be defensible is cutting it short at the best possible time, i.e. before it is too late. We can return to the Sandel quote with which we began to put flesh on this notion of 'before it is too late.' There is 'a relevant moral difference between aborting a foetus at a relatively early stage and killing a child' (Sandel 1996: 21) but it is not the one Sandel thinks. The difference is not that a human life has not begun but that, at least, it has not been allowed to continue for very long without being wanted. The moral difference between killing a child or, indeed, an infant and killing a foetus would be one of limits, between human beings whose very brief life one is allowed to cut short if you are not willing to look after them and human beings whose somewhat longer lives you are certainly not allowed to cut short no matter how much you would prefer not to have to look after them. One could see why even a humane or perhaps even an especially humane State might not be averse to giving its prospective parents what amounts to—what is *like*—a window of opportunity. However, it should be clear that the defense being developed now has a different range of application than the one developed earlier. It can be right that abortion be legal without that implying that every legal abortion is equally moral.

Our method of judging abortions can be further exemplified by considering the perspective of a third group: the doctors who perform them. In this case, too, it is worth following our procedure of asking what it is *like*, in this case to *be* an abortionist. In particular, is it best seen as *like* most other medical procedures? Current British law can stimulate reflection on this matter. It states that, within a specified time frame, in order for a woman to be allowed to have an abortion: 'Two doctors must decide that the risk to a woman's physical or mental health will be greater if she continues with the pregnancy than if she ends it' (Abortion Act 1967).

Although this puts formal responsibility in the hands of the doctors as if the decision to have an abortion can be decided much like other medical decisions, i.e. on grounds of health, just the fact that, apart from cosmetic surgery, it is hard to come up with any medical intervention that is designed to improve one's mental health makes it clear that this law only pretends to let doctors decide. In practice, conscientious doctors will do it so long as patients want it. The difference, then, from most medical procedures, is that most abortions cannot easily be seen as the consequence of medical advice.

Doctors are being put in the relatively unusual position, for them, of doing something at a patient's bidding. What is *this* like if it is not like most medical procedures? Doing what someone wants you to do for them because they want it rather than because they clearly need it is like doing them a favor. If the comparison is apt, while there is certainly nothing inevitably wrong with doing people favors, it does mean that thoughtful doctors, even those with no principled objections to abortions, should be free to think about their acts in the way we think about favors. Inherent in the idea of a favor is that it is a kind of special treatment. You do it just because they want you to, not because, since it can be shown to be needed by them, it becomes your duty to do it. Therefore, favors do always raise the potential question as to what extent, in the particular case, the treatment is merited. It follows that it would only be human and, I would add, justified for doctors to have opinions as to how admirable particular decisions to have abortions are.

The grammar they would be entitled to use in forming their opinions could be not the legality but the morality in the way developed above, of particular forms of abortion. I would certainly not suggest that this should ever lead conscientious doctors to say no when the legal criteria are met but I do think it could lead to justifiable feelings in doctors. While in many cases these feelings would be pleasure in being able to provide a valuable service, in other cases there could be feelings of irritation, reluctance, disrespect, maybe even repugnance. That such reactions could be justified is another way of seeing that, depending on what particular abortions are like, the act of abortion does raise moral as well as legal issues, now not only for those who decide to have one but also for those who are forced to perform one.

We have considered what various forms of abortion are like, what a State decision to legalize abortion is like, and what it is like to perform one. The remaining issue is what it is like to be the couple who have conceived in the world we have depicted, a world that is, in many respects, the contemporary western world. Although typically, the willingness to entertain the idea that abortion is like some forms of murder coincides with being against a woman's right to choose, in that we have defended the notion of offering couples a window of opportunity, clearly we can be said to be not denying the right to choose. The challenging issue, though, is what sort of choice this would be *like*.

Probably the most accepted current version of what it is like to have a choice is the one displayed in Anthony Giddens's analysis of what he calls 'pure relationships.' In these— his version of the way cutting edge contemporary persons think of their more committed sexual liaisons—'it is a social relation which can be terminated at will, and is only sustained in so far as it generates sufficient psychic returns for each individual' (Giddens 1991: 187).

To be able to choose in Giddens's sense is to be able to assess whenever one wants, even every day, whether one wants to stay in the thing or leave. The key, as he says, is to be able to *terminate at will*. This is not the choice that current abortion law or, indeed, current infanticide law allows with regard to conception and its upshot, foetuses. Instead of 'terminate at will,' one gets a brief chance to choose—to decide. After this brief period, there is no going back. This is choice, not as something that is always available, but as what comes and then goes. It is a brief period for deliberation, a make your mind up time. It is like the new version of chess that Wittgenstein imagined in which there was:

A rule by which each piece had to be turned around three times before one moved it. If we found this rule in a board-game we should be surprised and should speculate about the purpose of the rule. ('Was this prescription meant to prevent one from moving without due consideration?') (Wittgenstein 1958: par. 567, 150e-1e)

Choice in this sense is more like what marriage used to be like when, on the one hand it was no longer arranged by others but on the other hand divorce was not so easy or accepted. Hence the drama, whether heartbreak or farce, of last-minute cold feet, no doubt a reflection of the fact that one's choice to 'go through with it' was a fateful decision with life-long consequences. The possibility of abortion, if thought of in the way this chapter has been entertaining, offers couples this sort of choice.

As we certainly seem to be implying that the window of opportunity—a sort of pause when the couple get a chance to turn around in their minds, not a chess piece but what is about to happen—is a good thing, we should be able to say what appears good about it. Following the method used throughout, answering this question will require specifying what it is *like* to have this opportunity. But, as it seems wrong to depict what it is like to be a woman in this situation as the same as what it is like to be a man, for the first time in this chapter it does not seem right to ignore the undeniable biological fact that, though both genders are responsible for the conception, it is the woman who will, if they decide to go through with it, have to have the baby. As such, what seems good about the pause and the possibility of a legal abortion that it offers is that it lets the woman decide whether or not she is actually willing to have the baby. What would otherwise be inevitable can now be voluntary. What seems good here is that, even when being pregnant was not part of a plan, being forced into having a baby is still avoidable.

With regard to what it is like to be the man, how might the opportunity to pause be good for him given that, due to biology, no matter how willing *he* is, he cannot actually have the baby? There is still something he can give willingly. What he can give willingly is his support and it seems good, both for him that he have the chance to decide how much support he *is* willing to give and for her, that she be able to know, in advance, how much support she is likely to get because, of course, that could be a factor in how willing she might be to go through with it.

The one thing that could seem puzzling, even to men who understand their biological limitations and are committed to nothing being forced on anyone, is why, if they are supposedly able to have the opportunity to say how much support they are willing to give, they are *not* allowed to say that they are unwilling to give what is called, tellingly, child support, i.e. financial assistance for the child's upbringing. Whatever some men may argue, this limitation on their freedom seems good, however, because besides thinking about what it is like to be a woman or a man in this situation, we should also be thinking about what it is like to be the baby. If your mother is willing to have you even though she knows that your father is not, you could, even more than usual, fear for your future. It seems good, for your sake, that the person who is, after all, equally responsible for your conception should at least be required to support you financially even if he is unwilling to give the two of you any other form of assistance.

A key difference between standard discussions—whether pro or anti—and the approach taken in this chapter is that we have been able to avoid the seemingly factual but also, as Macintyre suggests, interminable because unresolvable issues that are currently exercising both sides in the debate. The most obvious example being whether or not abortion is murder. Unlike a fact, a metaphor cannot be *either* right or wrong but instead needs to be assessed in other ways. What makes the metaphor valuable is what it can reveal about the similarities and differences that, as we have argued throughout this book, are the actual way we come to grasp anything's identity. Hopefully, it has been shown that as we come to grasp a thing's identity—in this chapter the thing being abortion—even though we cannot claim to have discovered the empirically verifiable true facts about it, this is not to say we have not become somewhat better at judging it.

Notes

1   While I am solely responsible for this chapter's conclusions, I am greatly indebted to Eric Laurier, Allyson Noble, and Gregor Schnuer for a stimulating discussion of an earlier draft.
2   Hence some, in hearing his story, have remarked that who they really feel sorry for is the dog.

Chapter 5

Metaphors and the Issue of Incommensurability

The previous chapter was stimulated by some observations of Macintyre. But underpinning Macintyre's otherwise astute analysis of the difficulties that syllogistic reasoning about the pros and cons of abortion can embroil one in is a position we have directly opposed: he never even contemplates any alternative to the syllogism. Why does an alternative not occur to him?

Macintyre, understandably, expects that human action at the very least be intelligible. An unintelligible action, according to him, is one that refuses to obey the logic of a syllogism. If we can grasp his reasoning, it will enable us to shed further light on both the necessity and the desirability of our alternative method. Macintyre writes:

> We should be puzzled [...] by someone of whom we knew three things: first that he wanted to keep healthy, secondly that he had sincerely asserted *both* that to get cold and wet could be bad for his health *and* that the only way to keep warm and dry in the winter was to wear his overcoat, and thirdly that he habitually went out without his overcoat. (Macintyre 1985: 161, original emphasis)

What makes this person's actions unintelligible is that, given his major and minor premises, he really should be wearing his overcoat. As Macintyre recognizes, then, he is relying on Aristotelian logic for his diagnosis of unintelligibility. Therefore this example suggests to him that 'Aristotle's account of the practical syllogism can be construed as providing a statement of the necessary conditions for intelligible human action' (Macintyre 1985: 161).

The same form of reasoning about the requirements of intelligibility is also present in another example:

> I am standing waiting for a bus and the young man standing next to me suddenly says: 'the name of the common wild duck is *Histrionicus histrionicus histrionicus.*' There is no problem as to the meaning of the sentence he uttered: the problem is, how to answer the question, what was he doing in uttering it. (Macintyre 1985: 210)

As the first case remains unintelligible because we cannot identify a major and minor premise of this person that would make the act of not wearing an overcoat logical, this one is on the face of it unintelligible and can only become intelligible if we can identify a major and minor premise that could justify even such a strange act as this. For example, even though Macintyre is a total stranger to this man, perhaps (major premise) 'he has just come from a session with his psychotherapist who has urged him to break down his shyness by talking to strangers.' And (minor premise) the man worries what to say and the therapist had replied: 'Oh, anything at all' (Macintyre 1985: 210).

The only other way besides applying syllogistic reasoning that Macintyre has of making acts intelligible is by attributing apparently illogical actions to a failure of will. For example, it could still be intelligible that the first man is not wearing his overcoat in spite of his major and minor assumptions if, say, against his better judgment he cannot be bothered to remove the coat from a recalcitrant hanger. However, such an interpretation would work much better if Macintyre had not added the provision that the person acted this way 'habitually.'

It is this link between intelligibility and the willingness to apply syllogisms that leads Macintyre and, he thinks, all of us to impasses in deciding controversial issues. To return to the example that was the subject of the last chapter, whereas some might say that those who disagree with them by doing what they personally would never dream of doing—aborting a foetus—are acting unintelligibly, Macintyre would say: only if you cannot identify a major and minor premise that would make their act follow logically. And, for all the major issues of the day he has no trouble finding such premises. Thus whereas anti-abortionists, as we saw, think murder is wrong and abortion is murder, as we also saw, Macintyre imagines pro-abortionists thinking:

> Everybody has certain rights over his or her own person, including his or her own body. It follows from the nature of these rights that at the stage when the embryo is essentially part of the mother's body, the mother has a right to make her own uncoerced decision on whether to have an abortion or not. (Macintyre 1985: 6–7)

Between pros and antis: 'The rival premises are such that we possess no rational way of weighing the claims of one as against another' (Macintyre 1985: 8). Both sides have produced syllogisms according to which their actions follow and so, according to Macintyre, there is no way to decide between them. The two views are, as he later puts it 'incommensurable' (245, 246).

As we saw in the Introduction, other issues follow the same pattern. Fuller versions of the relevant syllogisms make his point even more clearly. Thinking about war (major premise): 'A just war is one in which the good to be achieved outweighs the evils [...] and in which a clear distinction can be made between combatants [...] and [...] noncombatants' (Macintyre 1985: 6). But (minor premise): 'In a modern war calculation of future escalation is never reliable and no practically applicable distinction between combatants and non-combatants can be made' (6). Hence, be a pacifist. On the other hand, don't because (major premise) 'the only way to achieve peace is to deter potential aggressors' (6). And (minor premise) 'you must build up your armaments and make it clear that going to war on any particular scale is not necessarily ruled out by your policies. An inescapable part of making *this* clear is being prepared to fight' (Macintyre 1985: 6, original emphasis).

Or, thinking about private versus public schooling and health services, abolish private schools and private medical care because (major premise) 'justice demands [...] equal opportunity' and (minor premise) 'no citizen should be able to buy an unfair share of such services' (Macintyre 1985: 7). But others, equally intelligibly, say definitely do not do these things because (major premise) 'everybody has a right to incur such and only such obligations as he or she wishes [...] and to determine his or her own free choices' (7). And (minor premise) abolishing private schools or medicine would violate this freedom.

Here we are rediscovering what we saw in the Introduction: Syllogisms only can offer effective judgments when their premises are definite and conclusive facts. As no one on any side of any of these controversies can muster any such fact, all seem equally rational and all end up talking past each other. We have said, though, that Macintyre does not end up criticizing the syllogism. Instead he offers another, many would say, a last-ditch, attempt to find 'the facts' and because of them, the one syllogism that all the disagreeing parties could agree is truly rational.

In order to understand Macintyre's own position, we need at least a brief excursion into the overall theme of his book. Far from attacking the proponents of these various syllogisms, Macintyre actually admires them. The basis of his admiration is that, even though they are failing to arrive at judgments that are not easily objected to by those with other premises, it is good that they are at least trying to find a rational basis for their judgments. What he is actually against are only those who have given up on this very project, in particular those he calls 'emotivists': 'Emotivism is the doctrine that all evaluative judgments and more specifically all moral judgments are *nothing but* expressions of preference, expressions of attitude or feeling, in so far as they are moral or evaluative in character' (Macintyre 1985: 12, original emphasis).

Or, to cite the version of emotivism for which he reserves particular scorn, there are some who say that whenever we try to argue that something is good we really are saying nothing more than 'Hurrah for this!' (Macintyre 1985: 12).

Macintyre proceeds to find various convincing grounds for dismissing emotivism. As the use of the notion that something has my personal approval is clearly distinct from the use of the notion that something is actually good, it is clear that those who believe, with Wittgenstein, that meaning is connected to use, could never accept collapsing the distinction between what is good and one's personal attitudes. The claim that something is good and the opposite: 'that is bad!' implies an appeal to an ... impersonal standard in a way in which 'I approve of this; do so as well' does not (Macintyre 1985: 19–20). And perhaps most telling, he suggests that all such an 'impoverished' (16) notion of the good really managed, was to characterize the defective morality of the Bloomsbury group who were its most enthusiastic supporters.

What he admires about the various proponents in the contemporary debates he cites is the fact that, unlike emotivists, they clearly are attempting to base their judgments on impersonal standards. Certainly, that murder is wrong, that persons have some rights over their own bodies, that a just war must produce more good than evil, that one should do what is necessary to preserve peace, that there should be equal opportunity for all, and freedom of choice all have this property. The difficulty with them is that all of these are premises that must be as factual as the statement that all men are mortal if the judgments derived from them are to be truly sound. As we saw in the Introduction and the previous chapter, even the idea that murder is wrong is not really a defensible fact. The same applies to all the other statements. Macintyre realizes this as well but instead of taking it as grounds to seek an alternative to syllogistic reasoning, he takes it as grounds to search for another premise, one that, in his view, *is* defensible fact.

Macintyre begins the key section of his book in which he proposes this fact and also various other supposed facts (in effect *his* minor premises) with a paraphrase of the well-known beginning of Aristotle's *Ethics*: 'Every activity, every enquiry, every practice aims at some good, for by "the good" or "a good" we mean that at which human beings characteristically aim' (Macintyre 1985: 148).

But what is important, as Macintyre himself states, is the distinctive way Macintyre interprets this statement:

> It is important that Aristotle's initial arguments in the *Ethics* presuppose that what G. E. Moore was to call the 'naturalistic fallacy' is not a fallacy at all and that statements about what is good [...] just are a kind of factual statement. Human beings, like the members of all other species, have a specific nature; and that nature is such that they have certain aims and goals. (Macintyre 1985: 148)

Once we know what this good we aim at is, we will know what Macintyre thinks the 'fact' about us is:

> What then does the good for man turn out to be? Aristotle has cogent arguments against identifying that good with money, with honour, or with pleasure. He gives to it the name of *eudaimonia* [...] It is the state of being well and doing well in being well, of a man's being well-favoured himself and in relation to the divine. (Macintyre 1985: 148)

The fact discovered then is that we all need to be *eudaimonia* (usually translated as 'happy'). As the supposed fact that murder is wrong leads, logically, to being anti-abortion in so far as abortion is murder, this fact can lead us to a logical judgment so long as we can decide what can produce *eudaimonia*. The additional fact that shows us the way is that 'the virtues are precisely those qualities the possession of which will enable an individual to achieve *eudaimonia* and the lack of which will frustrate his movement toward that *telos*' (Macintyre 1985: 148).

Just as the major premise that murder is wrong and the minor premise that abortion is murder could seem to allow us to judge abortion as illogical and therefore unintelligible for anyone with such beliefs (unless they suffer a failure of will), the major premise that our good is *eudaimonia* and the minor premise that it is the virtues that produce *eudaimonia*, could seem to allow us to judge virtuous behavior as the only logical and therefore intelligible behavior of persons with such beliefs, so long as *their* will power suffices.

By developing a syllogism that makes virtuous behavior seem intelligible, Macintyre has managed to find a rationale for attempted forms of behavior, i.e. behavior that tries to be just, temperate, wise, and courageous, that is to say behavior that attempts to conform to the cardinal virtues. These behaviors are rational because they supposedly lead to what we all supposedly want, happiness. Also, the minor premise can be and has been expanded, not least by Macintyre himself, in order to make intelligible other forms of behavior, e.g. self-knowledge and constancy, by assuming that these, too, lead to happiness (Macintyre 1985: 241, 242). As such, Macintyre deserves credit for being one of those who has supplied a cogent critique of the misleadingly limited and even harmful version of what the good could be, put forward by the emotivists. However, his claim to have discovered not just a premise but a fact, the claim that, as we have seen, his attempt to maintain syllogisms as the definitive method for arriving at judgments ultimately depends on, surely cannot be accepted. It seems even less likely that Aristotle has discovered the true basis of human happiness than that it can be definitely shown that murder is always wrong. Thus even an author such as Charles Taylor (1989), who is clearly influenced by the way Macintyre has managed to redefine the good, makes the obvious point that Macintyre's actual proposal amounts to a highly suspect form of nostalgia that utterly fails to acknowledge the progressive aspects of modernity and postmodernity.

There is, however, a problem that such a criticism of Macintyre has tended to obscure. As this criticism either simply ignores or accepts as unavoidable the incommensurability problem that he was right to raise, the critic is no better than he is at being able to resolve it. One way to see what we are trying to do in this book is to suggest a way out of the impasse that is created for syllogistic reasoning by the fact of competing, equally tenable assumptions. We say it is only the requirements of syllogistic reasoning that make it necessary to decide the truth of assumptions.

Our alternative way of judging was displayed in the previous chapter in how we reworked the ideas of abortion being murder and murder being necessarily wrong. Instead of embarking on the futile task of deciding whether abortion is murder and the equally futile task of deciding whether murder is wrong, tasks only required by the need of syllogistic reasoning to have premises, we tried instead to decide what abortion and murder are like. While it is true that we did not end up with the sort of judgments syllogisms purport to produce: abortions must be wrong, abortions must be right, it surely cannot be said that we did not manage any form of judgment. We were able to judge in the sense of *evaluate* various forms of abortion and, at the same time, various forms of murder.

An important question, not yet addressed, is where this form of judgment leaves the purported facts that the users of the syllogism, whatever their views on abortion, were so insistent on. While we have denied both that one can say that murder is necessarily wrong and that abortion is not necessarily murder, we have *not* denied either that abortion is like at least some murders or that some of the murders that abortion is most like may not be as bad as other murders. One reason these admissions are significant is that they can be brought to bear on the incommensurability problem. Once it is realized that abortion is not like every form of murder, one might be somewhat more likely to be less disapproving of at least some abortions even if one has a very strong belief in the evils of murder. At the same time, once it is realized that abortion may be like some forms of murder, one is likely to be somewhat less disapproving of at least some arguments against it. The two opposing views are no longer as clearly and necessarily incommensurable as Macintyre leads us to believe.

That we have a viable alternative way of judging that helps with the incommensurability problem would be much more convincing if it can also be demonstrated for Macintyre's other examples: persons who are convinced that abortions must be allowed because of rights over one's own body, pacifists versus proponents of deterrence theory, and believers in equal opportunity versus advocates of private schools and medicine.

First, returning to the subject of abortion, we now need to analyze what was not considered in the last chapter, namely what abortion might be like if it is justified by the idea that everybody has 'certain rights over his or her body' and there is a stage 'when the embryo is essentially part of the mother's body' (Macintyre 1985: 6). As a start—it being odd to insist on the right to cut off parts of anyone's body, even one's own—it is worth trying to work out what kind of body part an embryo is being pictured as like according to this argument. Even those most firmly pro-abortion might find unsettling what might well be the most plausible comparison: It seems embryos are being treated with no more respect than tumors.

As Macintyre is careful to couch this position in terms of the rights of male as well as female bodies, it also seems worth considering what it would be like for males to treat what could be the closest equivalent to what females have that is 'essentially part of their bodies' in this way. Have any but the most irresponsible male types ever suggested they should be free to decide when, where, and how to dispose of their sperm?

It does seem, then, that in order to resist thinking of the embryo as like a tumor or males as having irresponsible forms of freedom, it is best to imagine the embryo, even at a very early stage, as part of someone else's body, albeit the kind of part that is utterly dependent on the person carrying it for its survival, growth, and overall well being. However, it must be stressed that seeing it this way does not imply that one should not have the right or, even, dare we say it, the responsibility to, in some cases, dispose of it at an early stage. For example, to return to an argument that was made in the last chapter, if, on reflection, one feels unwilling or unable to do what would clearly be necessary to continue to care for it, might not abortion, at the legally permissible stage, be a valid right? In terms of the incommensurability issue, then, one does not actually need to go so far as to claim that an embryo is part of one's own body (a claim that 'the other side' is bound to dispute and a claim that could never be proven because it is not a fact) in order still to think that abortion should be a woman's right.

Turning to a second issue Macintyre discusses, if it is accepted that neither pacifists nor deterrence theorists have definite facts on their side, what becomes of their arguments? Macintyre's modern-day pacifists say that a just war is one in which good outweighs evil but, as that can never happen in a modern war because too many non-combatants will be killed, no war is just. As the one thing that appears clearly evil in this scheme is the death of non-combatants, we need to work out what a just war, in this vision of it, would be like. It seems, at first, that a just war would be any war with not too many civilian casualties, but that would seem to make a just war too much like a war of conquest, so long as it is conducted humanely. It is highly unlikely that this is what pacifists mean to be advocating.

Instead, their idea must be, in line with conventional understandings, that a just war is one that one's own side does not start. Not starting it is what gives one's side the conviction that fighting it, whatever the costs, is 'good.' But, pacifists proceed to argue, the conditions of modern warfare make even this defense of war untenable. There are likely to be so many innocent casualties that even a war someone else starts is not worth all (the inevitable evil) of the fight.

We can already detect a closer affinity to the arguments of deterrence theorists than Macintyre has led us to expect. The deterrence theorists are no more interested in starting a war than the pacifists but they think that the only way to stop what, in Macintyre's attempt to articulate their point of view are called 'potential aggressors,' is to 'build up your armaments' (Macintyre 1985: 6). We need to consider, in line with our method, what such tactics are like. Clearly they are different from merely doing enough to defend yourself. They amount instead to trying to intimidate—threaten—all those 'potential' aggressors with the overwhelming negative consequences of any attack they might contemplate.

What both pacifists and deterrence theorists have in common, then, is that both think they have found the way to avoid starting a war, the former by an unwillingness to fight no matter what, the latter by seeking to intimidate anyone who might try starting one. But just having this idea in common could still make their positions irreconcilable until it is realized that not only do they have the same goal, they are also making (different but comparable versions of) the same mistake. They resemble each other. Both leaving oneself utterly vulnerable to attack—the clear consequence of pacifism—and seeming to threaten 'potential' adversaries—the clear consequence of the arms build-ups associated with so-called deterrence—are equally adept at *creating* adversaries. The former do it by becoming much too tempting a target for absolutely anyone with even a minimal interest in expansion, the latter by convincing too many others that they really are confronted with a threat. It can even be said that what they both have in common is that, in spite of their good intentions to never themselves start a war, this could be precisely what they (in a sense) manage, the former by a stance that virtually invites others to attack, the latter by making others so frightened of them that they might well decide that the only defense against them is a pre-emptive strike.

In that it now seems both that the two sides have the same goal and are also making the same mistake (unwittingly acting in ways that could start a fight), while it is a stretch—given, if nothing else, likely differences in temperament—to expect them to easily agree on what in particular to do, it can still be said that at least a productive discussion rather than incommensurability could loom. What would be productive would be seeking to work out, as a way to assuage valid fears on both sides, what would be enough armament to make it likely one could defend oneself and so not mislead others into thinking one was as tempting as a lamb to a wolf but, at the same time, what would constitute not so much armament that one could seem to be threatening others.

What to make of Macintyre's attempt to show that a commitment to justice is incommensurable with a commitment to freedom? In this case, the supposed facts about justice are (major premise): 'Justice demands every citizen should enjoy, as far as possible, an equal opportunity to develop his or her talents and his or her other potentials' (Macintyre 1985: 7). And (minor premise) 'requisite for such equal opportunities includes the provision of equal access to health care and education' (7). Therefore, justice requires 'abolishing private schools and private medical practice' (7) as these are obviously not institutions all have equal access to. The supposed conundrum arises because freedom would certainly seem to require *not* abolishing these two institutions.

However, as a start, it is worth noting that this issue is not as divisive in actual current discussions as the others Macintyre has raised. Even those with the most resolute commitment to equality of opportunity have not tended to propose actually abolishing private schools or private medicine. By the same token, even those with an equally resolute commitment to freedom have, over time, tended to see the justice of many measures that clearly have increased equality of opportunity, such as abolishing gender, racial, and ethnic discrimination and, latterly, some movement toward positive discrimination.

But how rational are the judgments that have led those strongly committed to either justice or freedom not to fight on this terrain? In so far as our method of judgment remains helpful, it will be relevant to consider what it would be *like* to seek to promote equality of opportunity in the way that is producing controversy. What is most striking is the difference between this tactic of abolishing private medical care and schooling and the more accepted ways of promoting equality of opportunity just noted. Whereas the other ideas are ways of *removing* barriers that have obstructed equal opportunity for some groups, e.g. the exclusion of blacks, women, or other groups from certain educational or career paths, this idea is more like *creating* a barrier for one group, i.e. those rich enough to actually want to pay for education or medical care. Hence, Macintyre is right to see such a proposal as a restriction on freedom.

But is it also as necessary, as he assumes, to foster equality of opportunity? While there might well be ways in which it is necessary to restrict the freedom of some to further the opportunities for many, on reflection, it is not really clear that these proposals are like that. The trouble (for the argument that what justice requires and what freedom requires in this case inevitably conflict) is that it is not at all likely that abolishing private schools or medicine would improve public provisions in these realms and so achieve the admittedly worthy aim of developing the 'talents [...] or [...] other potentialities' (Macintyre 1985: 7) of those unable or unwilling to spend their money in this way. That one thing disappears would not necessarily make the other thing any different, much less any better.

If this meant that those other than the rich are therefore doomed never to have the same chance to realize their potential, then the need to restrict the rich in this way might still arise, but it can be suggested that there *are* ways to improve public education and medicine that, besides not advantaging the rich, at the same time cannot legitimately be objected to by them as infringements on their freedom. One obvious example that applies to Macintyre's country of origin, the United Kingdom, is that one could abolish the tax breaks—based rather implausibly on their claim to being a charity—now given to private schools. Such a move could well improve public education (by releasing more potential funding for it) but, at the same time, it would be ludicrous for anyone to claim that makes them less free to attend private schools. In this instance, as in the other cases we have so far discussed, it seems clear that what seemed an impossible dilemma is better seen as a false dichotomy. This is not to say hard choices are not necessary, in this instance between indulging the rich versus treating them somewhat more harshly by removing one of their little perks, but to admit that there are hard choices is not like facing incommensurables.

Macintyre offers one more story of apparent incommensurability. He invents two characters, A and B:

A, who may own a store or be a police officer or a construction worker, has struggled to save enough from his earnings to buy a small house, to send his children to the local college, to pay for some special type of medical care for his parents. He now finds all his projects threatened by rising taxes. He regards this threat to his projects as *unjust*. (Macintyre 1985: 244, original emphasis)

On the other hand:

B, who may be a member of one of the liberal professions, or a social worker, or someone with inherited wealth, is impressed with the arbitrariness of the inequalities in the distribution of wealth, income and opportunity. He is, if anything, even more impressed with the inability of the poor and the deprived to do very much about their own condition as a result of inequalities in the distribution of power. He regards both these types of inequality as *unjust*. (Macintyre 1985: 245, original emphasis)

Unlike the previous case, there seems no conflict here between the demands of freedom and those of justice. Both A and B seem committed to justice. Instead the potential conflict stems from their different priorities for justice: A being more interested in protecting his projects, B in helping the poor.

However, actors can have different priorities without that resulting in anything so extreme as incommensurability. Macintyre recognizes this:

It is clear that in the actual circumstances of our social and political order A and B are going to disagree about policies and politicians. But *must* they so disagree? The answer seems to be that under certain types of economic condition their disagreement need not manifest itself at the level of political conflict. If A and B belong to a society where economic resources are such, or are at least believed to be such, that B's public redistributive projects can be carried through at least to a certain point without threatening A's private life-plan projects, A and B might for some time vote for the same politicians and policies. (Macintyre 1985: 245, original emphasis)

The supposed incommensurability only arises when times are hard:

But if it is, or comes to be, the case that economic circumstances are such that either A's projects must be sacrificed to B's, or *vice versa*, it at once becomes clear that A and B have views of justice which are not only logically incompatible with each other but which [...] invoke considerations which are incommensurable with those advanced by their adversary party. (Macintyre 1985: 245)

What accounts for the incommensurability? Not exactly total dismissal of the validity of the other's projects. Instead:

A holds that principles of just acquisition and entitlement set limits to redistributive possibilities. If the outcome of the application of the principles of just acquisition and entitlement is gross inequality, the toleration of such inequality is a price that has to be paid for justice. B holds that principles of just distribution set limits to legitimate acquisition and entitlement. But if the outcome of the application of the principles of just distribution is interference—by means of taxation or such devices as eminent domain—with what has up till now been regarded in this social order as legitimate acquisition and entitlement, the toleration of such interferences is a price that has to be paid for justice. (Macintyre 1985: 245–6)

It is certainly true that A and B would be at loggerheads in this case but we must remember that what Macintyre is seeking to demonstrate is not potential for conflict but the incommensurability that can afflict, in this instance, justice itself.

If we stop thinking of justice as a fact or, in this case, two competing beliefs leading to logically incompatible conclusions, we become free to ask what A and B are imagining justice as like. Macintyre can actually help us here, though it is with an observation that he only makes in passing:

We may note in passing [...] that in the case of both A's and B's principle the price for one person or group of persons receiving justice is always paid by someone else. Thus different identifiable social groups have an interest in the acceptance of one of the principles and the rejection of the other. (Macintyre 1985: 246)

While A and B do apparently have different principles they also have at least one thing in common. This one thing can be formulated as their sense of what both of them think justice can be like: it can be like a situation in which the price is always paid by someone else.

But what can be suggested is that, even though Macintyre is right that such a view might be consistent with their interests, it may not be consistent with a credible view of what an interest in *justice* could be like. In fact, McHugh's recent analysis of justice can be utilized to suggest that the very idea that only someone else should pay the price is fundamentally at odds with much of an interest in justice. He speaks of justice as 'the sole virtue that requires sharing' (McHugh 2005: 140). Or, in the same vein, that 'justice forms the conduct that delivers sharing or fails to do so, indeed justice *is* that conduct, for good or ill' (140, original emphasis). That is, perhaps sharing may not be good but still to not commit to it is, in effect, to not commit to justice at all. As to what must be shared for justice, it 'encompasses each of life's collective occasions, *including those that make us suffer*' (150, original emphasis).

Clearly Macintyre has managed to invent an occasion that could make us, i.e. A and B, and not just them but also the poor, suffer but the crucial point that can be derived from McHugh is that if A, B, and also the poor are not willing 'to share in the suffering' one has to doubt that, whatever their interests, they can be seen as having much interest in justice. The rule of thumb here would be that what is really incommensurable would be an interest in only *other* people paying the price and an interest in justice. Or to put it positively, when there are difficult circumstances for a collective such as those Macintyre imagines, an interest by that collective in justice would require that *everyone* in it pay (at least part of) the price. In practice, even in the sort of circumstances Macintyre imagines, this would probably mean that no matter how much inequality there might be, *everyone* must do what it takes, including endure some sacrifices to make sure the inequality is not 'gross,' while no matter what sacrifices A types might be asked to make, they could not be so disproportionate as to include devices like eminent domain.

Now that we have looked at several examples of the method of comparison at work, it may help to reiterate what was said earlier in an effort to explain why this method can help with the incommensurability problem. The key is that it no longer is necessary to totally reject the principles one holds dear in order to have some sympathy for an opponent's position.[1] For example, one who firmly believes that one has rights over one's own body can potentially have more sympathy for opponents of abortion once it can be seen that these opponents need not be denying that such rights exist because their position can be based on realizing how different a foetus is from most parts of one's body. Similarly, once firm believers in equality of opportunity can see that the sort of barrier that not being able to attend a private school represents is significantly different from the other obstacles, such as gender and racial barriers that they have (rightly) supported the removal of, they can have more sympathy for those who (in the name of freedom) have objected to the removal of this particular barrier.

The point that syllogistic reasoning can create the mistaken impression of incommensurability can also be addressed from the perspective of well-known disagreements as to the requirements of logic. Macintyre, as a follower of Aristotle, would assume the validity of what is called the 'law of the excluded middle'. This states that if X is true, not-X cannot also be true. In our material, Xs could be the various beliefs that apparently make believing the various not-Xs, which are other beliefs that appear opposed to X, impossible in the sense of contradictory.

In logic that derives not from Aristotle but from Hegel, it is argued that it can sometimes be possible to 'rise above that logic' that excludes the middle (Birchall 1981: 75). What we rise above is the assumption that everything must fit 'the formula of either-or' (75). For example, any 'middle' is excluded when it is thought that *either* one believes that abortion is murder *or* one becomes a strong advocate of abortion. Any 'middle' is also excluded if it is thought that *either* one believes that an embryo is part of a woman's body *or* one becomes a strong opponent of abortion.

Put in these terms, we have been arguing that the 'middle' does not have to be excluded. We have done so, for example, by suggesting how there need not be a contradiction between believing that abortion does have at least some similarities to some forms of murder and not being totally opposed to it. Also, we suggested that there is not necessarily a contradiction between being reluctant to accept that an embryo is that similar to parts of a woman's own body and still not opposing all forms of abortion. That the two 'middles' here need not be excluded is another way of saying that apparently opposing beliefs are not necessarily incommensurable.

Note

1   Syllogistic reasoning, on the other hand, forces one to reject out of hand any conclusions whose premises appear to contradict one's own. For an analysis of how syllogisms enforce such a restriction, see Blum 1974: 112–5.

Chapter 6

Israel and Palestine

S yllogisms purport to enable one to decide whether doing X is good or bad in the sense of right or wrong. But in so far as apparently equally valid syllogisms leading to opposite conclusions are available, the actual effect is just that persons starting from differing premises become equally convinced that they are right and others are wrong. There are obviously other divisive phenomena besides the ones discussed in the last two chapters. Can a change from syllogistic to metaphoric reasoning help toward a resolution of any of these cases as well? This chapter will utilize the method of metaphor to suggest a possible way forward for a situation that is certainly no less divisive than the abortion debate: the current conflict between Israelis and Palestinians.

As in the case of abortion and also the other issues raised by Macintyre, if one attempts to resolve the outstanding issues with syllogisms, all that happens is that each side can argue that what they want to happen is the good in the sense of the logically correct outcome. Thus, Amos Oz describes how the Palestinians see the issue as follows:

> The Palestinians are in Palestine because Palestine is the homeland and the only homeland of the Palestinian people. In the same way in which Holland is the homeland of the Dutch, or Sweden the homeland of the Swedes […] The Palestinians have tried, unwillingly, to live in other Arab countries. They were rejected, sometimes even humiliated and persecuted, by the so-called Arab family. (Oz 2004: 5)

Translated into a syllogism: Every people deserve a homeland (major premise). If we Palestinians cannot live in Palestine, we will not have a homeland (minor premise). Therefore this is *our* home.

But here is the issue as the Israelis see it:

> The Israeli Jews are in Israel because there is no other country in the world which the Jews, as a people, as a nation, could ever call home. As individuals, yes, but not as a people, not as a nation […] The Jews were kicked out of Europe. (Oz 2004: 5)

Translated into a syllogism: Every people deserve a homeland (same major premise). Like the Palestinians, we Jews have no other possible home (minor premise). Therefore, this is *our* home.

Both sides can convince themselves logically that they are the ones that belong there. It is also true that in this case there is a third view. For many years outsiders have watched what is happening, appalled, and have felt sure that *they* have the solution, a solution that eludes both sides because they are too partisan to see it. Jacques Derrida provides a typical example of this third view. Faced with the awkward dilemma of having accepted an invitation to speak in Israel while not wanting his presence to be construed as a statement in support of just the Israelis, Derrida declared:

> With all the gravity this requires, I wish to state right now my solidarity with all those, in this land, who advocate an end to violence, condemn the crimes of terrorism and of military and police repression, and advocate the withdrawal of Israeli troops from the occupied territories as well as the recognition of the Palestinians right to choose their own representatives to negotiations now more indispensable than ever. (Derrida 1991: 39–40)

In these negotiations one precondition is the continued existence of 'the Israeli state (whose existence, it goes without saying, must henceforth be recognized by all and definitively guaranteed)' (Derrida 1991: 40).

We see here his attempt to not choose sides. The Israelis get what they want: an end to terrorism and a guaranteed state. The Palestinians get what they want: negotiations and an end to the repression that characterizes the occupation. Expressed as a syllogism: An end to violence is what is good (major premise). No more terrorism by the Palestinians or repression by the Israelis defines the end of violence. What will end the violence is the end of occupation and the guaranteed existence of Israel (minor premise). Therefore all these things are what should happen.

But, while according to this syllogism, all the violence from both sides seems illogical, Israelis can and will easily reply that it is only the repression of the occupied territories that is 'guaranteeing their existence' while at the same time Palestinians can easily reply that it is only the terrorism that provides a realistic hope of ending the occupation. What seems logical to both sides then is exactly what does not seem logical to Derrida, namely to continue fighting with each other.

But what if, instead of seeking to derive logical conclusions from various apparently credible facts, we seek a metaphor for a situation in which two parties are locked into a seemingly endless struggle in which, since both are equally convinced they are right, for seemingly rational reasons they can never stop fighting with one another? What if, in other words, we seek to discover what such a situation is *like*? Oz writes:

> I don't believe in a sudden burst of mutual love between Israel and Palestine. I don't expect that, once some miraculous formula is found, the two antagonists will suddenly hug one another in tears in a Dostoyevskian scene of long-lost brothers reconciled [...] Unfortunately I don't expect anything like this. I don't expect a honeymoon either. If anything, I expect a fair and just divorce between Israel and Palestine. (Oz 2004: 21–2)

While divorces are rarely pleasant and often do amount to a kind of defeat, here the prospect of one appears as a stimulating thought; a breath of fresh air. This is because what can be good about a divorce is that in a situation where a couple really and clearly cannot stop fighting with each other, where they cannot live together happily, they do not need to merely preserve that utterly unsatisfactory status quo, or end up oppressing and/or terrorizing one another, even killing or being killed by one another, as they perhaps would have had the possibility of divorce not been invented. The idea that divorce has invented is that they can, instead, stop trying to live *together*.

To the obvious objection that, while they are certainly unhappy living together as witnessed by the fact that they really cannot stop fighting, the Israelis and Palestinians are not exactly a married couple, we say that, perhaps without fully realizing it, Oz has come up with another example of what we have been developing with the help of various authors throughout this book. We have another metaphor, a stimulating comparison that can aid us in visualizing a situation and also to arrive at a judgment as to what can be done about it. In this case the judgment would be that, while it remains the case that the Israeli and Palestinian views are at such loggerheads that they seem destined to just carry on the current hostilities, that is *not* the only inevitable or even logical result because warring parties in this day and age do have another option. It can be in both their interests to arrange something *like* a 'fair and just divorce.'

Even as we accept that Oz's metaphor is highly illuminating, it should, however, be noted that its relevance is only demonstrated by his managing to show that there are more similarities between the Israelis and Palestinians and couples who agree to divorce than either of the two peoples currently realize. Crucially, Oz has a way of suggesting to both sides that, once they realize what the other side is *not* like, they will at the same time see, like a divorcing couple, that 'it is not a struggle between good and evil'; it is 'a clash between one very powerful, deep and convincing claim and another very different but no less, powerful, no less humane claim' (Oz 2004: 4–5). He does this work by explaining that each side is confusing the other with someone else. In the case of the Palestinians, they need to stop confusing the Israelis with colonialists. Or, as Oz puts it:

In much contemporary Arab literature [...] the Jew, especially the Israeli Jew, is often pictured as an extension of the white, sophisticated, tyrannizing, colonising, cruel, heartless Europe of the past [...] Very often Arabs [...] fail to see us as we really are—a bunch of half-hysterical refugees and survivors, haunted by dreadful nightmares, traumatized not only by Europe but also by the way we were treated in Arabic and Islamic countries [...] Israel is indeed one large Jewish refugee camp. (Oz 2004: 18–9)

Similarly, the Israelis need to stop confusing the Palestinians with Nazis:

By the same token we, Israeli Jews don't see the [...] Palestinians, as what they are: victims of centuries of oppression, exploitation, colonialism and humiliation. No, we see them as pogrom-makers and Nazis, who just wrapped themselves in koffias and grew moustaches and got sun-tanned, but are in the same old game of cutting the throats of the Jews for fun. (Oz 2004: 20)

Remedying these confusions are essential because only if *these* comparisons were apt would keeping the fighting going or even a struggle to the death rather than a divorce be the best way forward.

Furthermore the Israelis must see that, while they are not exactly a colonial power, they are like one side of a couple who should divorce because they cannot live together in peace. Relevant here are the unpalatable truths uncovered in recent times by a small group of Israeli revisionist historians.[1] They provide evidence of the extent to which the Palestinians who left Israel during and after Israel's War of Independence were, in effect, forced to leave by the Israelis. Similarly, the Palestinians must come to see that they too, *are* like the other half of a couple who really do need to separate because they have been equally reluctant to do what is necessary to live in harmony with the Israelis. As Oz describes the necessary self-understandings that each side must achieve, in this regard concerning the now homeless Palestinian refugees:

> There is a deep disagreement on where to put the blame, or most of the blame, for this tragedy. You will find some modern Israeli historians who put the blame on Israel. I suppose in a few years eventually, and I hope to live to see this day, you will find some modern Arab historians who will put the blame on the Arab governments of that time. (Oz 2004: 31)

In other words, once enough time has passed to enable a reasonably fair-minded view of the events, it will be realized that the actions of *both* sides during the period when they were sharing the land have amply proved their own unwillingness or inability to do enough to accommodate the needs and desires of the other so as to make living together happily an at all realistic possibility. In various ways ranging from outright force to a clear reluctance to treat the others as equals, both sides indicated that the others were far from welcome and what they really wanted was just for them to go away. As such, they are perfectly suited to a divorce.

Besides using his idea that the two sides could arrange something like a divorce to argue that the conflict is not insoluble and can even result in an outcome that both sides could accept as fair, Oz also manages to use the idea to indicate something of the nature of the possible agreement that needs to be arrived at: 'Divorces are never happy even when they are more or less just. They still hurt, they are painful' (Oz 2004: 22).

As in a just divorce, on the part of both sides: 'what we need is a painful compromise' (Oz 2004: 9). Both sides, then, cannot expect to be exactly happy with the outcome. Both will have to willingly undergo the pain of giving up something they would prefer to keep, precisely because they have proved unable to live together in harmony.

In detailing the nature of the compromise, he goes on to explain why this one may even be somewhat more painful than most divorces because of one way in which it is *not* like the typical divorce. As we imagine a divorce, one major plus is that the warring parties no longer have to endure the pain of living together. In this case, though, neither one of them has anywhere else to go. So, it is as if

> the two divorcing parties are staying on in the same apartment. No one is moving out. And as the apartment is very small, it will be necessary to decide who gets bedroom A and who gets bedroom B and how about the living room [...] Very inconvenient but better than the kind of living hell which everyone is going through in that beloved country. (Oz 2004: 22–3)

What can be derived from the metaphor, then, is the idea that when a space cannot be shared by two groups who both have rights to it, there is still hope because there can be an equitable division. Oz even offers an additional metaphor for what he thinks will ensue after the equitable division: 'Once this divorce is conducted and a partition is created, I believe Israelis and Palestinians will be quick to hop over the partition for a cup of coffee together' (Oz 2004: 24).

That is, after the divorce and in line with the fact that, unlike most divorcees, they will still be living in close proximity to one another, they will be in a position to act *like* good neighbors do.

Returning now to the attitude of third parties such as Derrida to the conflict, in addition to his main metaphor, Oz offers a further stimulating comparison that manages to recast the nature of the conflict. Derrida's approach implied that further fighting was hard to understand because it was illogical. Consistent with this, it is true that most outside observers, even including those who have actually tried their hands at helping the two sides negotiate a peace settlement, have ended up losing patience with them. The consensus is that both sides are just acting irrationally. Without exactly contradicting this consensus, Oz does have a very relevant comparison to make:

> Of one thing I can assure Europeans: our conflict in the Middle East is indeed painful and bloody and cruel and stupid, but it's not going to take us a thousand years [...] We will be faster than you were, and shed less blood than you did [...] Be a little more careful in wagging your fingers at all of us. Our bloody history is going to be shorter than your bloody history. (Oz 2004: 24–5)

In judging an event or thing, besides formal metaphors, there are more straightforward forms of comparison. As with Searle's description of Sally as detailed in the Introduction, certain features of things such as tallness only get their identity in comparative form. We do tend to think, because the Israeli–Palestinian dispute has been going on for over sixty years and because it is still unresolved even though one peace agreement—the Oslo Accords—was signed fully 19 years ago, that the conflict is just dragging on and on, leading more and more persons to start to believe it may never be satisfactorily resolved. However, if we remember how long some other conflicts have taken before they were settled, if we *compare* it to similar situations, we can come to see that there is a compelling case to be made that sixty years is not really a very long period of time.

In this chapter, rather like the Dante chapter, we have been hugely dependent on the perspective of just one person, Amos Oz. It is worth reflecting on why it might be that he has more to offer than other figures, equally knowledgeable and equally engaged in this Middle East problem. Arguably the most relevant fact about him is that he is, by trade, a novelist. As such what he possesses, above all, is an *aesthetic* sensibility. This means that like Dante, like the authors of fairy tales, and like great painters, his is the skill of being able to visualize the nature of a situation by finding similarities and differences, the very skills of one who can come up with appropriate metaphors rather than devoting their efforts and energy to deriving apparently logical conclusions.

It is true that the kinds of judgments that are produced about various forms of action in Dante's work, or concerning abortions and now about a long-standing international conflict are not so clear-cut as the use of logic can promise. Nothing seems clearly or exactly right or wrong. At the same time, though, this form of judgment does seem to offer a different sort of promise, the promise of finding some common ground where only opposing positions hitherto seemed possible.

Note

1   See, for example, Morris 1987.

Chapter 7

The Problem of Evil

Much of the previous discussion has led to the conclusion that the key to developing moral judgment is to be able to appreciate what an action, e.g. hypocrisy, seduction, abortion, abolishing private school, immigration to Israel, etc. is like and unlike. In this chapter, there will be a shift of emphasis. Might it also be the case that those who make very faulty moral judgments are those who have trouble seeing what things are alike and unalike? Pursuing this question requires finding a case of someone who was clearly evil.

While we could return to Dante for examples, in our time, Hannah Arendt deserves the most credit for clarifying the nature of the problem of evil. She has inspired this chapter. Her basic insight is well captured in the subtitle of the book in which she reports her discovery: 'the banality of evil.' She writes of her book's subject, Adolph Eichmann,

> pointing to a phenomenon which stared one in the face at the trial […] Eichmann was not Iago and not Macbeth, and nothing would have been farther from his mind than to determine with Richard III 'to prove a villain.' Except for an extraordinary diligence in looking out for his personal advancement, he had no motives at all […] With the best will in the world one cannot extract any diabolical or demonic profundity from Eichmann. (Arendt 1965: 287)

However Eichmann committed evil, it was not by willing it. Probably Arendt's clearest example concerns his role in the event the Nazis were concentrating on before they began mass extermination, a policy of mass expulsions. Eichmann was in charge of the Austrian branch of this in which close to 150,000 people were expelled. The question then, if Arendt is right about him, would be how he could do this without actually willing evil. We begin to see how both he and Arendt reach this conclusion when we get a fuller picture, first of some events that had occurred before Eichmann arrived in Austria:

> Immediately upon his (Eichmann's) arrival, he opened negotiations with the representatives of the Jewish community, whom he had first to liberate from prisons and concentration camps, since the 'revolutionary zeal' in Austria, greatly exceeding the early 'excesses' in Germany, had resulted in the imprisonment of practically all prominent Jews. After this experience, the Jewish functionaries did not need Eichmann to convince them of the desirability of emigration. Rather, they informed him of the enormous difficulties which lay ahead […] The chief difficulty lay in the number of papers every emigrant had to

assemble before he could leave the country. Each of the papers was valid only for a limited time, so that the validity of the first had usually expired long before the last could be obtained. (Arendt 1965: 45)

Because it will prove important to how he manages to interpret his role, we note both that Eichmann did not need to convince the Jews as to what was desirable and that it is they who were telling him of difficulties. Both these facts can be seen to feature in how he interprets his subsequent action. According to him:

He and his men and the Jews were all 'pulling together,' and whenever there were any difficulties the Jewish functionaries would come running to him 'to unburden their hearts,' to tell him 'all their grief and sorrow,' and to ask for his help. The Jews 'desired' to emigrate, and he, Eichmann, was here to help them. (Arendt 1965: 48)

Clearly, if all he was doing was helping them to realize their desire, it makes sense for him to conclude that he was not willing any evil. But to understand all that is at stake here, we need to know exactly what this 'help' and fulfillment of the Jews' 'desire' are referencing.

Eichmann proudly explains that his reference is to his idea of 'an assembly line, at whose beginning the first document is put, and then the other papers, and at its end the passport would have to come out as the end product' (Arendt 1965: 45, quoting Eichmann's testimony).

Arendt explains that he put this into practice by having

all the officers concerned—the Ministry of Finance, the income tax people, the police, the Jewish community, etc. [...] housed under the same roof and forced to do their work on the spot, in the presence of the applicant, who would no longer have to run from office to office. (Arendt 1965: 45)

This, then, is how he supposedly fulfilled their desire and helped them by resolving their difficulties.

Assuming that it remains evil to have a major role in the rapid expulsion of nearly 150,000 citizens from their homes, we need to work out what can produce such evil if it is not an evil will. Arendt's way of seeking to understand Eichmann is to further articulate her notion of the banality of evil. She suggests: 'It was sheer thoughtlessness—something by no means identical with stupidity—that predisposed him to become one of the greatest criminals of that period' (Arendt 1965: 288).

It does seem right that someone who interprets his idea of the assembly line form of expulsion as merely fulfilling someone else's desire and resolving all their problems is not thinking very hard about their own actions. But can we become more precise about what such lack of thought entails? Arendt offers further help: 'He *merely*, to put it colloquially, *never realized what he was doing*' (Arendt 1965: 287, original emphasis).

Yes, but how can one not realize what one is doing? It is, suggests Arendt, in a phrase that clearly resonates with that flaw having something to do with his banality, a 'lack of imagination' (Arendt 1965: 287).

She tries to develop what he would need to imagine but cannot by suggesting that a 'decisive flaw in Eichmann's character was his almost total inability ever to look at anything from the other fellow's point of view' (Arendt 1965: 47–8).

On the one hand it is surely right that it would have helped if Eichmann had realized how his actions were being interpreted by the Jews as well as by himself. For example: *They* could not possibly think of being expelled from their country as what they actually desired. It is equally right that at least one aspect of imagination is to adopt others' viewpoints as well as one's own. However, might there be more to having an imagination than Arendt could be leading us to believe here?

In general in this work we have been highlighting persons who are able to *imagine* stimulating comparisons. We can now propose that there could be an analogous problem of people who cannot see the similarity between things just because these two things have a slightly different appearance. To suffer from this inability does sound like a lack of imagination. An example of two things that have slightly different appearances is the appearance of the threat of force as distinct from the actual use of that force. Not seeing the fundamental similarity between 'merely' threatening force and actually using it is what is leading Eichmann to the absurd conclusion that the Jews, who of course only 'want' to leave because they are facing a severe threat, actually desired to leave. So being unable to imagine *this* similarity could account for one case of him not being able, as Arendt puts it, to realize what he is doing.

Another example of two things that have slightly different appearances are, on the one hand finding something one does not wish to do difficult and on the other hand finding what one *still* does not wish to do a little easier. If one cannot imagine how similar these can be, one could be convinced that one is helping someone just because you are making the inimical easier. Lack of imagination of these two similarities, then, could be what makes Eichmann's conclusion that he is helping the Jews possible.

If this is what lack of imagination is like, then we can perhaps be more precise about what form the presence of imagination (as displayed in previous chapters) would take. It would either be being able to see similarities even between things that have much more obvious apparent differences than say, force and the threat of force, or being able to see differences between things that in terms of appearance are quite similar. One has the imagination to notice a potential similarity between things that, from the perspective of their appearance, seem somewhat distinct, or to notice a significant difference between things whose similar appearance will lead to some confusion between them. Good metaphors, what we have been calling stimulating comparisons, would be cases of the former.[1]

It can also be suggested that at least one of Arendt's examples of what she means by the illumination provided by 'the other fellow's point of view' indicates that it is because seeing another's point of view can often help with either of these feats that she associates it with imagination. So proud was Eichmann of his ability to realize the Austrian Jews' desire by his idea of the assembly line that he summoned some German Jewish functionaries to admire his achievement:

> They were appalled. 'This is like an automatic factory, like a flour mill connected with some bakery. At one end you put in a Jew who still has some property, a factory, or a shop, or a bank account, and he goes through the building from counter to counter, from office to office, and he comes out at the other end without any money, without any rights, with only a passport on which it says: You must leave the country within a fortnight. Otherwise you will go to a concentration camp.' (Arendt 1965: 46)

Their point of view is a valuable aid to the imagination of anyone wishing to realize what Eichmann might be said to be doing here because, whereas he was misled by the minor difference in appearance between force and the threat of it to not be able to grasp their fundamental similarity, these people are *not* misled by the apparent differences between baking bread and this way of treating human beings, into noticing the similarity between how Eichmann and his colleagues are treating the Jews and how bakers treat bread.

The ambiguity in appearances could seem to lead only to confusion in so far as we wish to arrive at judgments. One does not have the security that clear-cut facts provide but it can also be treated as what makes room for imagination. There is scope for imagination because it is no longer necessary to take every apparent difference seriously and because it is necessary to be alert to potential similarities even where serious differences are apparent. That imaginative work does result in not taking some differences seriously, and finding some similarities where serious differences do exist would be what gives such work an unserious, i.e. a playful quality, a quality that, while we have not made it a topic as yet, may be evident in many of our previous examples. It can also be what makes such work controversial among those suspicious of the playful, as we shall now see.

Like Macintyre, Martha Nussbaum is someone who wishes to defend Aristotle. However, her defense emphasizes not his promotion of syllogistic logic but his development of 'the method that announces appearance-saving as its goal' (Nussbaum 1986: 241). Given what has just been developed concerning the appearance–imagination relation, it seems unlikely that this particular version of Aristotle will allow for an adequate appreciation of any exercise of the imagination since imagination requires ignoring at least some apparent differences and similarities. As such, it will be worth looking at the way Nussbaum develops her defense of Aristotle. She does it by an extremely negative assessment of various attempts by his predecessor, Plato, to include metaphors as a major tool in his method of theorizing.

One case she cites is when, in Book IX of *The Republic*, Plato has Socrates compare some human activity to what cattle do:

> Nor have they ever tasted stable and pure pleasure, but, like cattle, always looking downwards and being over the earth and their tables, they pasture, grazing and mounting,

and, for the sake of getting more of these things they kick and butt one another with iron horns and weapons and kill one another through their insatiability. (Plato: ll.586a–b, quoted in Nussbaum 1986: 154)

About this passage, Nussbaum remarks:

This may seem grossly unfair. Surely, one might wish to argue, the pursuits of a species must be assessed from within the ways of life and standing needs of that sort of creature. If you are such that the typical member of your species looks to you like a member of another species different from yours, then you are not the sort of ethical judge we want or need. Value simply *is* radically anthropocentric, and it should not count against a pursuit that the reasons for choosing it are not evident to a creature who is, or has become, different in nature from those for whom it is a good. (Nussbaum 1986: 154–5, original emphasis)

With her insistence on the need for only species-specific judgments by typical members of those species, one wonders who Nussbaum thinks Plato is being grossly unfair to. Us? Cattle? Both? Whereas we said metaphoric reasoning can have a playful quality, these remarks have the opposite feel. They seem humorless. The humorless feel probably stems from Nussbaum, as part of her mission to save appearances, apparently thinking that she needs to remind us (and Plato) that there are actually serious differences between how we humans behave and how cattle do. The danger in such a reminder is that it is blinding us to the stimulating discovery that could make this metaphor seem appropriate: Yes, there are many differences between us and cattle, but if all we are intent on are mundane concerns, we *are* rather like them in one respect: we are both *always looking downward*. This is not unfair to cattle because, given that is their limit, it is no criticism of them. As for us, while it is obviously a criticism of some of us or all of us at least some of the time, it would only be unfair if we really cannot afford to spend or would not benefit from spending at least a little more time looking up. Here, by thinking she must devote all her energy to saving the appearances, in this case the different appearance of a grazing animal and, say, a businessman who never thinks about anything but making money, Nussbaum fails to appreciate a potentially valid way to visualize and hence judge some forms of activity that, if not exactly evil, are surely less than the best we can do.

Another example is Nussbaum's critique of Plato's use of an itch metaphor. In this case, it will be more convenient to present Plato's point of view before we turn to Nussbaum's objection. Plato had an understandable concern with the relation between things being pleasurable and them being valuable. On the one hand, if anything gives us pleasure it is hard to argue that it lacks value, while on the other hand one does not want to say that the pleasure of the thing is the only or even the best measure of its value. A particularly difficult case is anything that gives great—very intense—pleasure. Surely, one feels like arguing, any such pleasure must be of immense value.

In the late dialogue, *Philebus*, Plato has Socrates speak of a man experiencing such pleasure that 'he even leaps for joy, he assumes all sorts of attitudes, he changes all manner of colours, he gasps for breath, and is quite amazed, and utters the most irrational exclamations' (Plato 1970: ll.47a–b, 93).

Further elaborating this great—this intense—experience, Socrates suggests this man

> will say of himself, and others will say of him that he is dying with these delights [...] of all pleasures he declares them to be the greatest; and he reckons him who lives in the most constant enjoyment of them to be the happiest of mankind. (Plato 1970: ll.47b–c, 93)

We of course imagine that the pleasure Socrates has in mind here is sex but it turns out that what he is actually talking about is when we are scratching an itch.

As he noticed that cattle, unlike us, have to keep their heads down, now he is noticing that, if our only criterion for the value of a pleasure is how great its magnitude—its intensity—is, we get into the absurd position of having to argue that it is when we are scratching an itch that we are having an experience that is about as valuable as it can get. However, if we merely realize that he is not talking about sex here, we miss the point. Instead: though there are of course many differences between sex and scratching an itch, although, then, they *appear* very different, it is possible to notice one way in which they are alike: they can both make us moan—scream—die—with delight. This similarity is quite important because it should make us realize that, while it might seem that the most reliable way to assess the value of our sex life is by how much moaning and groaning it produces, that is problematic because it seems too much like assigning great value to itch scratching.

Nussbaum's response to the itch metaphor has the same properties as her response to the cattle metaphor. As we got a lecture on how we are a quite different species from cattle, now we get a lecture on how different sex is from scratching an itch: 'From the internal viewpoint of the ordinary human being the central appetitive pursuits are in important ways *not* like itching and scratching' (Nussbaum 1986: 153, original emphasis).

As these 'important' differences apply to sex:

> Most of us [...] do not pursue sexual activity merely as a source of release from a painful tension; it is connected with other complex ends such as friendship, self-expression, and communication. There are reasons why most of us do not take the option of becoming eunuchs. (Nussbaum 1986: 153)

This works as a list of some of the many differences in how sex and itching appear. The list no doubt helps to explain why, unlike Plato, 'most of us' would never dream of comparing them. But, unless what Nussbaum means by self expression and communication is something close to moaning and groaning, she misses the point that her version of what 'in fact' sex *is* like for most of us makes it not like the very kind of sex that Plato warned us against being prone to overvaluing, namely sex that seems incredibly worthwhile just because it offers a similar kind of ecstasy to what we get from scratching an itch. As with the cattle metaphor, Nussbaum gets so offended by the proposed similarity that she does not see the force of the critique. In the former case the critique being that we look down too much, in this case the critique being that we are too inclined to assign great value to things merely because of the magnitude or intensity of pleasure they offer, irrespective of any assessment of worth.

It is important that Plato's critique of measuring value by sheer magnitude of pleasure be understood because otherwise we really are in danger of overvaluing any activity just because it gives us a considerable magnitude of pleasure. Nussbaum makes exactly this mistake. As part of her effort to make clear that there is more to the pleasurable life than itching, Nussbaum ends up defending the value, not just of sex. She endorses the fact that, according to her, we

> praise those who are capable of entering into [...] activities in a way that endows them with intrinsic value: the gourmet, the connoisseur of wines, the person who can treat a sexual partner as an end in him or herself, rather than as a mere means to a state of null tension. (Nussbaum 1986: 153)

While it is not completely false to observe that some of us admire wine connoisseurs and gourmets, surely the more apposite observation about such people is the one Plato was getting at: as the sort of pleasure that people like this can offer us is one that can only be measured by criteria like immediate intensity and magnitude, their contribution should be recognized to be only of limited value.[2] Probably even some gourmet chefs themselves sense this. Hence Britain's Jamie Oliver broadening out to an effort to save America's children and even the less ambitious Hugh Fearnley-Whittingstall commencing a campaign to improve the lives of chickens.

Dante would surely be a case in point but are there contemporary theories in which not taking every apparent difference too seriously, while also discovering similarities even where there are apparent differences, is a major factor in gaining protection from doing wrong? Particularly if, as it should be, seeing differences even among apparently quite similar appearances is included as an additional part of the activity, this approach is one way to interpret the theorizing of Blum and McHugh. For example, one of their works has as its focus the difference between merely following rules and being principled (Blum and McHugh 1984). Given how much effort they devote to distinguishing these two modes of action, they could not deny that they *appear* quite similar. At the same time, in that they suggest that someone who does not manage to differentiate them will not even think s/he needs to *consider* whether any action of theirs is worth doing, because the merely rule-guided actor 'only wants to do it because it is expected' (Blum and McHugh 1984: 117), we can say that appreciating the difference between following rules and following one's principles would lessen the chance of some forms of evil actions occurring, It would ensure that at least the actor him/herself must find some value in an act before undertaking it.

Other examples of the same method can be found in both Blum's and McHugh's solo work. Like Nussbaum, Blum has offered an assessment of one of Plato's metaphors from *The Republic*. The passage the metaphor occurs in is when Socrates is beginning to depict the diet of the inhabitants of his imaginary just city. Glaucon objects that the fare is 'pretty plain' (Plato 1976: ll.372c, 121). Socrates then adds things like 'salt, of course, and olive oil and cheese, and different kinds of vegetables from which to make country dishes' (Plato 1976: ll.372c, 121).

But Glaucon is still not happy: 'Really, Socrates, Glaucon commented, that's just the fodder you would provide if you were founding a community of pigs' (Plato 1976: ll.372d, 122).

What Blum takes from this is that

in the city of pigs, the absence of desire reflected in the absence of spices is essentially the absence of any drive for quality or for bringing out the best of things [...] In the absence of such desire, [...] [while it] seems to be a healthy city, but for Plato [it] is not a city at all. As he implies, his city of pigs is a pigpen and not a city. (Blum 2011: 87)

On the one hand, Blum acknowledges that such a city does *appear* to be healthy but such an appearance pales into insignificance once one realizes, with Plato, that such a city has an uncomfortable resemblance to what might be on offer in a pigpen. Blum, then, disregards certain superficial similarities. He is also, of course, unlike Nussbaum, disregarding the differences that would make the comparison less discomfiting, i.e. the obvious differences between pigs and even members of our species without what Blum calls the drive for quality.

It is worth noting that, in order to meet Glaucon's criticism, Plato has Socrates introduce various forms of pleasure into his city:

It will want couches and tables and other furniture, and a variety of delicacies, scents, perfumes, call-girls and confectionery. And we must no longer confine ourselves to the bare necessities of our earlier description, houses, clothing and shoes, but must add the fine arts of painting and embroidery, and introduce materials like gold and ivory. (Plato 1976: ll.373a, 123)

It is actually the people who live like *this* who are much later in *The Republic* compared to cattle. Nussbaum's objection that Plato simply does not realize how valuable activities like gourmet foods, wine tasting, and sex are because these activities can be pleasurable in themselves, would be much more credible if he had not *revised* his conception of what some of us are like—cattle (because of looking downward, i.e. confining ourselves to mundane interests) but (because we do appreciate refined things) not exactly pigs—precisely so as to *include* as part of the life he is critical of, a life devoted only to the sort of things that Nussbaum thinks he does not understand the nature of.

The paper already referred to by McHugh on justice can provide another example of the Blum and McHugh approach (McHugh 2005). The paper does not deny that, because it is a form of equal treatment by attempting to disregard race or gender, opposition to affirmative action can *appear* to be just. For example, it looks much more like justice than, for example, early practices of racial segregation or, indeed, legalized slavery do. But it can still be theorized as unjust because nowadays it amounts to another, even if apparently just, way to perpetuate grossly disproportionate opportunities for some groups in society. The general idea again is that it can be seen to be crucial to not be distracted by apparent similarities, in this case between injustice and affirmative action, and to appreciate the affinity between apparently quite different things, i.e. previous efforts to produce equality of opportunity by trying to abolish discrimination and current efforts to do the *same* thing by a limited form of positive discrimination.

Inspired by Arendt's idea that evil is not the product of will but the product of persons' banality—their lack of imagination—this chapter has specified the form that this lack takes as a failure to appreciate some similarities and some differences. Adolf Eichmann; those who cannot see the similarities between a type of sex and scratching an itch; those who cannot see the difference between a healthy life and how pigs live; and those who cannot see the difference between affirmative action and discrimination, were all interpreted as suffering from one or another species of this problem.

Having seen various positive and negative examples of judgment, we should at this point be in a position to put some flesh on Arendt's initial idea, as mentioned in the Introduction, that judgment is like the aesthetic virtue of good taste. Hans-Georg Gadamer remarks:

> Taste is defined precisely by the fact that it is offended by what is tasteless and thus avoids it, like anything else that threatens injury. Thus the contrary of 'good taste' actually is not 'bad taste'. Its opposite is rather to have 'no taste'. (Gadamer 1989: 36–7)

The absence he has in mind would involve what we have been detecting as an inability to detect differences. Without taste, too much appears the same. One is indiscriminate, unable to discriminate.

It is true that in normal usage we are not so inclined to treat an ability to see likenesses as also a component of taste. Perhaps this is because we derive our version of taste in the sense of discernment from Leibniz's principle of the identity of indiscernibles. According to him:

> There is no such thing as two individuals indiscernible from each other. An ingenious gentleman of my acquaintance […] in the presence of […] the Princess Sophia […] thought he could find two leaves perfectly alike. The Princess defied him to do it, and he ran all over the garden a long time to look for some, but it was to no purpose. (Leibniz 1956 [1717]: 36)

So long as there is more than one leaf, it is right that one will be able to discern *some* differences between them. However, Hegel laughs at this as a method for working out a thing's, even a leaf's, identity:

> The story is told that when Leibnitz [*sic*] propounded the maxim […] the cavaliers and ladies of the court, as they walked around the garden, made efforts to confute the law […]

Their device was unquestionably a convenient method of dealing with metaphysics—one which has not ceased to be fashionable. All the same, as regards the principle of Leibnitz, difference must be understood to mean not an external and indifferent diversity merely, but difference essential […] Likeness is an Identity only of those things which are not the same, not identical with each other. (Hegel 1892 [1816]: 218)

Hegel is making fun of persons who think they can solve the question of a thing's identity by empirical means. One cannot because identity, e.g. of two leaves, signifies likeness among things that are admittedly *not* the same.[3] Good metaphors, of course, have this property. Discernment as a part of good taste in a sense that owes more to Hegel than Leibniz would include not just the ability to see differences but the ability to see likenesses in things that are admittedly not the same.

Besides the motivation—its association with moral judgment—that has already been offered for cultivating and exercising this faculty, a more general point can now be made. To be able and willing to be discerning is desirable because it is a way of going beyond sense impressions—empirical observations—without being at all dismissive of this realm. One is not denying sense perceptions but one is doing more than just looking at what is there, more than taking it at face value. When one can connect what looks different and differentiate what looks the same, one is no longer merely looking—not just perceiving. In addition, one deserves to be called perceptive.

Notes

1   Hence we can conclude that Dante, especially as displayed in *The Inferno*, and Eichmann represent polar opposite examples of the same principle. The former, due to his strong imagination, is highly sensitive to evil. The latter, with his absence of imagination, is oblivious to evil.
2   Dante made a similar point in his treatment of 'gourmets' in Purgatory.
3   Hegel here supplies another version of what is wrong with Ricoeur's conception of sameness as mentioned in the Introduction.

Chapter 8

Tragedy vs Comedy

The previous chapter has begun to suggest that the ability to detect some similarities and some differences can give us a surprising power, the power to avoid and to see the roots of some forms of evil. We have also associated this faculty with being discerning. Whereas some, notably Eichmann, might really lack this power, it is likely that others might have it without being motivated to exercise it. This seems odd: Why not do something that seems so desirable? What this chapter will suggest is that there is a downside to understanding that we have this power and that can explain at least some forms of resistance to exercising it.

Nussbaum will again provide the example, this time because we will be trying to understand why, though she balks at seeing similarities between us and animals, she is quite happy to argue strongly for another comparison, our resemblance to a plant. At the very start of her book, she quotes with approval a passage from the Greek poet, Pindar, in which, at least in her interpretation, we are like a plant. Pindar wrote: 'But human excellence grows like a vine tree, fed by the green dew, raised up, among wise men and just, to the liquid sky' (Nussbaum 1986: 1).

According to Nussbaum this metaphor works because 'the excellence of the good person [...] is like a young plant: something growing in the world, slender, fragile, in constant need of food from without' (Nussbaum 1986: 1).

And as she further elaborates, we are like it because 'it needs fostering weather (gentle dew and rain, the absence of sudden frosts and harsh winds), as well as the care of concerned and intelligent keepers, for its continued health and perfection' (Nussbaum 1986: 1).

Even Nussbaum admits that the comparison, unlike say those we have found in Dante and elsewhere, is hardly likely to immediately strike a chord with us: 'If this picture of the passive vine tree begins to strike us as incompatible with some aspiration we have for ourselves as human agents [...] there is the consolation that, so far, Pindar has apparently left something out' (Nussbaum 1986: 2).

Nor, we would add, is it just anything that is left out as, after all, even much more compelling metaphors than this one leave things out. Nussbaum, to be fair, recognizes if not the only at least a glaring version of what the comparison would seem to ignore. She points out that 'however much human beings resemble lower forms of life, we are unlike [...] in one crucial respect. We have reason' (Nussbaum 1986: 2).

That we, unlike plants, possess the ability to make use of reason is undeniable and one cannot help thinking this difference would be significant enough to spoil the metaphor, but before we accept this conclusion we need to look at how Nussbaum defines reason. According to her, that we can reason means 'we are able to deliberate and choose, to make a plan in which ends are ranked, to decide actively what is to have value and how much' (Nussbaum 1986: 2).

This is an oddly limited version of what reason can do. Thus, while it does appear to differentiate us from plants, it is much less clear that it would even differentiate us from many animals. Think for example of a cat clearly intent on going outside until it finds out that it is raining and decides to stay inside instead. This cat certainly is choosing and might even be said to be deliberating, e.g. if it hesitates before opting to go back inside. But what reason can do, *if it is defined in this way*, is enable Nussbaum's analysis to take a surprising turn. If *this* is the 'rational element,' 'it seems possible that this rational element in us can rule and guide the rest, thereby saving the whole person from living at the mercy of luck' (Nussbaum 1986: 2).

We would be unlike plants if reason could save us from being at the mercy of luck, i.e. freed, unlike them, from contingency, from sudden winds and harsh frosts. But since reason, whatever it can do, certainly, especially in her version, *cannot* do this, we are back to the idea that we are like plants, after all. Both of us are always in danger of being buffeted, destroyed even, by unfortunate circumstances beyond our control.

As this supposed resemblance between us and plants does depend on such an odd picture of what reason can at its best do, i.e. totally remove us from the threat of contingencies, therefore enabling us to conclude it cannot do its work, i.e. remove contingencies, it is worth considering what is grounding such a view of reason. What will be suggested is that Nussbaum has a way to transform this limited version of reason and the weakened picture of the human condition that it leaves us with, i.e. that we are not all that different from plants, into a kind of strength.

First, she says that with this picture of the human condition, as with plants, when looking at a person and their relation to events the focus will be on 'what does not happen through his or her agency, what just *happens* to him' (Nussbaum 1986: 3, original emphasis).

But though this is consistent with seeing us as having no more agency—no more power—than plants, how might it become, however implausibly, a sign of our strength? Nussbaum herself notes that such a version of us could leave us with 'a raw sense of the passivity of human beings and their humanity in the world of nature, and a response of both horror and anger at that passivity' (Nussbaum 1986: 3).

Why the horror and anger? The following passage begins to explain:

That I am an agent, but also a plant; that much that I did not make goes toward making me whatever I shall be praised or blamed for being; that I must constantly choose among competing and apparently incommensurable goods and that circumstances may force me into a position in which I cannot help being false to something or doing some wrong; that an event that simply happens to me may, without my consent, alter my life; that it is equally problematic to entrust one's good to friends, lovers, or country and to try to have a good life without them—all these I take to be not just the material of tragedy but everyday facts of lived practical reason. (Nussbaum 1986: 5)

No matter how much I try to reason (in her sense), all these problems will occur. It follows that life—everyday life—can be seen as composed of the material of tragedy. So the horror and anger arise as we contemplate the potentially *tragic* nature of our lives.

However, as Nussbaum is interpreting us as not just as powerless as plants but as highly susceptible to tragedy, we still face the question of what is behind her seeing us in such a weak and negative way. We have already noted that Nussbaum is another theorist who is strongly influenced by the perspective of Aristotle. We know, of course, that one of the things Aristotle has analyzed in some detail is the nature of tragedy. There is evidence that it is accepting his version of tragedy that could explain how Nussbaum manages to transform a both limited and seemingly negative view of our lives into something positive. Thus, as she notes: 'Aristotle has a high regard for tragedy. Both in the *Poetics* itself and in the *Politics* discussion of young citizens, he gives it a place of honour, attributing to it both motivational and cognitive value' (Nussbaum 1986: 378).

While she does not really explain the basis of this high regard, in order to avoid merely accepting Aristotle's word as law (rather like many did in medieval times), we need now to explore, at least briefly, why he assigns such a high value to tragedy, both as a motivational and cognitive tool. According to Aristotle, all literature must 'represent men in action' (Aristotle 1958: 1448a, 5). Individual authors, though, must decide what sort of persons to represent. They must either 'be superior or inferior, either better or worse than those we know in life' (1448a, 5). It is partly the character of authors themselves that determines what sort of representation they will opt for: 'The more serious minded imitated the deeds of noble men; the most common imitated the action of meaner men' (1448b, 8).

There are, then, two fundamentally different types of literature. The way we tell the difference between them is whether they deal with those who are 'superior', 'noble', 'morally worthy', or, on the other hand, the 'inferior', the 'common;' the former attributes apply to tragedy, the latter to, in Aristotle's version, comedy. Even though tragic figures are passive, fragile, and lacking in agency and, even though their lives cannot be said to produce good outcomes, still we can see how they could, seen in the way Aristotle distinguishes them, deserve to be highly regarded. At least they appear superior, noble, and morally worthy. That is to say, at least they are not common, mean, and generally inferior. If your actions can be said to be tragic, at least you cannot be accused of being comic, comedy being understood by Aristotelians as 'an imitation of men who are inferior [...] the ludicrous is a species of ugliness' (Aristotle 1958: 1449a, 10).

Here we have a sense of why Nussbaum, for one, may be content to treat us, when things go wrong, as essentially tragic figures. We do not, if we are tragic, suffer the embarrassment of being comic. However, it is important to note that Aristotle's version of comedy is highly problematic. Even if it must be conceded that there would be something at least slightly ridiculous about anyone whose action is comic, this is not to say that all or even most such actions are ludicrous, ugly, or even at all ignoble. Below we will try to develop a more balanced assessment of what it can be like to be a comic figure. However, there is a much more pressing issue: No matter how ridiculous and even ludicrous some comic figures might be, can understanding how they come to act as they do provide a clearer explanation of how evil can occur than Nussbaum's view of evil as the tragic consequence produced by how limited our power of reason is?

The most compelling evidence that there might indeed be some relation between comedy and outright evil is provided by a further aspect of Arendt's diagnosis of Eichmann. Besides finding him lacking in imagination and thoughtless, she also, almost in spite of herself, has to admit that she actually finds him funny. Of his taped testimony to the police, she writes that it 'constitutes a veritable gold mine for a psychologist provided he is wise enough to understand that the horrible can be not only ludicrous but outright funny' (Arendt 1965: 48). Or, again: 'His cliché-ridden language produced on the stand, as it had evidently done in his official life, a kind of macabre comedy' (4).

In the previous chapter we tried to make Arendt's idea of Eichmann more precise by suggesting that what she called his thoughtlessness and lack of imagination took the form of an inability to recognize extremely obvious similarities, e.g. between the effect of force and the effect of the threat of force, and extremely obvious differences, e.g. between really helping someone and just removing an obstacle standing in the way of an unwelcome fate. Now we can suggest that it is right to see something comic here; the comedy of someone who seems, unaccountably, to be blind to the presence of what is so obviously there—in the first case an all too clear similarity, in the second an equally clear difference. Furthermore, while it is admittedly appalling and therefore rightly horrifying to the visiting Jewish functionaries, the assembly line processing of the Austrian Jews mentioned in the last chapter can be seen as another case of the Nazis, including Eichmann, seemingly unable to recognize a difference that is all too obvious. That is to say, while it is horrible, it is also laughable because it elides a too obvious difference when someone invents a process that treats a human being in the way a loaf of bread should be treated.

Do our other examples of wrongdoing also have a comic element? We have no other examples of persons failing to recognize such obvious differences and similarities as does Eichmann, which is to say no one else's mistakes are comic in the sense of ludicrous. That this is so makes sense in that all our discoveries of similarities and differences must not have been totally obvious as they did require some theorist's imaginative work before they became transparent. However, to the extent that, even in retrospect, we can come to appreciate that we were failing to see a similarity that we do have the ability to see, e.g. between flattery and having dung come out of our mouths, or failing to see a difference that we also have the capacity to see, e.g. between following a rule, even well, and being principled, that can make us feel that we have been a bit of a fool. We are comic in that we were not able to see something—a difference or a similarity—that is there to be seen. It is quite a different sort of mistake from the one Oedipus makes in that, at least in Sophocles' (tragic) version of the story, there is no way he could have had the ability to see the similarity between Jocasta and his mother.[1]

Seeing actors as comic rather than tragic leads to a different view of human agency. When things do not work out according to plan, Nussbaum thinks that means we need to think of it as what just happened as opposed to what we do or make. But from a comic perspective, the fact that one does not plan it does not mean that there is not still the possibility that one has a major role in making it happen. As this applies to the type of actor Nussbaum focuses on, ones who seem to be doing something good, in so far as their 'plan' involves them in a major mix-up that we are satisfied human understanding is such that they could have had the power to avoid, any bad results are not accurately seen as just totally outside their control—their power as agents. For example, when Socrates suggested that the residents of his just city should have only figs for desert, he certainly was not planning the result that people would be living like pigs. But, if we accept Glaucon's and Blum's analysis of what would be happening, we must agree that Socrates *makes* this happen by excluding more luxurious deserts. In Blum's terms, he makes it happen by mistaking an overly puritanical life for a healthy one. Similarly, if a person who is convinced that he is just finds himself accused of supporting policies that discriminate against blacks, while this would clearly not be his plan, it could still be an event he has a major role in making happen.

He makes this happen if we can understand, with McHugh, that this person is confusing justice with policies that are flawed because they do not allow some equitable modification in supposedly neutral standards that, when not modified to take account of the innumerable disadvantages blacks face, serve merely to perpetuate de facto discrimination.

So-called good actors certainly do not have total control. There are many bad outcomes that really do 'just happen' to them, but they do have more potential control than Nussbaum leads us to believe. We can see that in the comic, because avoidable, mistakes they make, i. e. not seeing relevant differences or similarities that lead to unplanned negative outcomes.

Nussbaum devotes hardly any attention to the opposite case: actors who we are quite confident are doing bad, even evil, things; but if her only explanation for the unplanned things that can happen to people who seem good is that these things just happen, it is unlikely that her explanation for the bad things that bad people do would be that *these* things just happen. Probably the only thing that she could imagine these people not planning is getting caught. But if we can begin to see such people as essentially fools, then we can also begin to see how even outcomes that seem very obviously a result of their actions might not be part of their plan. As seen by Arendt, this is certainly the case for Eichmann. He is so mixed up about what would really consist in helping someone that he appears to be authentically surprised that the Jews who testified at his trial were not exactly grateful to him. Even when he heard what they actually said about him, he assumed they must be changing their tune because 'when "times have changed so much," the Jews might not be too happy to recall this "pulling together" and he did not want "to hurt their feelings"' (Arendt 1965: 48). He just cannot see that, no matter what he thought, what he did was clearly not seen as help by the Jews.

Even if one is, unlike Nussbaum and Aristotle, not biased against comedy, it needs pointing out that seeing the comic side of an outcome, particularly if it undeniably inflicts considerable damage on someone who is, by all accounts, an innocent victim, is not the most natural reaction. Instead, the natural reaction would be to be both shocked and dismayed at the ability of evil actors to get their way, to accomplish their ends. The clear vulnerability that such events demonstrate should and often does lead to the deep question of whether good even is actually better than evil. Therefore, even people whose upbringing is such that they would never go so far as to go over to the other side can easily become bitter and demoralized, bitter that their continued adherence to standards seems not to offer the rewards of the alternatives those standards define as evil, demoralization taking the form of a loss of enthusiasm for all the actions that are supposed to be good.

A crisis of confidence in victims, then, is the natural response to the fact that evil acts are perfectly possible. Both how natural such a response is and how the kind of reflection we have been calling seeing the comic side can help to restore confidence in what is good, can be seen from Arendt's anecdote about the Jewish functionaries and their reaction to Eichmann's assembly line expulsions. Surely part of what appalled them was the ease with which such a horrible crime could be committed. The ability to do evil, then, is clearly a form of power. And yet by finding something downright ludicrous about Eichmann's procedure, something clearly laughable about it; by reflecting, then, that only a fool would act that way, have they not managed to weaken the attraction of evil and so restore their inevitably shaken confidence in the conviction that good is better after all?

But not only is it not natural to see the comic element in such events. It is not necessarily easy. Another example may clarify this point. Imagine a tourist being pickpocketed on holiday. It is certainly not natural to treat this as a laughing matter. Furthermore, it is hard to see how, even if one has the inclination, one can. It cannot be suggested that the funny mistake is the act of robbery because that is clearly no mistake on the perpetrator's part and, furthermore, the ease of its accomplishment and the clear benefits that ensue can make one legitimately wonder what, apart from what the conventions tell us, is exactly wrong with being a successful pickpocket. If, though, it could, on reflection, occur to the tourist that he is being treated like a sort of particularly generous ATM machine, this could at once help him see that there is something both laughable and mistaken about the act and restore his conviction that it might be better, after all, not to be a pickpocket.

What alternative to a bitter and demoralized response to the undeniable presence of evil is on offer here? The possibility of being what we could begin to describe as a good-humored person could characterize anyone with the ability to find good reasons to laugh at even serious acts of evil. The good humor can be explained as achieved by the ability to find evil laughable. One finds it laughable by managing to find foolish mistakes of the type we mentioned above—mistakes of similarity and difference—that have produced the act. By seeing foolish mistakes, one manages not to be jealous or bitter toward those who do such acts. Hence one's good humor.

The meaning of good humor in the sense intended here itself can be the subject of confusion and so it needs to be distinguished (our method again) from some similar ways of responding to evil, which, I would argue, are *not* defensible ways to restore confidence. Seeing the funny side is different from the optimism of seeing the bright side in that seeing how evil is mistaken is different from trying to find some good that will come out of it. Good humor is also different from the philosophy associated with Leibniz that we live in 'the best of all possible worlds' because 'even particular evil and individual suffering played an essential role in the total harmony' (Torrey 1946: IX). As Voltaire shows by satirizing this position in *Candide*, this view has to rationalize everything, in effect never facing the fact that anything that happens can actually be bad (Voltaire 1946 [1759]). As has hopefully been made clear, to find a way of laughing at an actor because s/he cannot tell the difference between things that are clearly not at all the same or cannot detect similarities when they are clearly present does not at all justify their action because the laughter can affirm rather than deny that it was the wrong and even a terrible thing to do.

Note

1   Here we get a glimpse of why, as I think is the case, unlike the other metaphors we have discussed, Nussbaum's does *not* seem playful. Whereas the others ignore differences they know exist, e.g. between us and cattle, or meaningful sex and itches, Nussbaum seems blind to differences that do exist, i.e. between our powers and the powers of plants.

Chapter 9

Teaching

It can be quite humiliating to realize one is mixing two or more things up. For one thing, it rules out any claim to being a particularly superior person. No matter how serious the outcome, one seems, as the last chapter suggested, more comic than tragic. However, there is at least one positive consequence of seeing our major flaw as a tendency to confuse things. If a state of confusion is the position we are in, it may be that all we need to learn is how to distinguish or relate things that we already benefit from having some knowledge of. We do not need to start from scratch. We do not need to learn everything.

There is a passage in Aristotle that has a relevance to this proposed connection between what does and what does not need to be taught and the activity of only needing to see differences and similarities. He is complaining about one method of attempting to identify the Sun. According to Derrida, who cites the passage, the complaint is that

> he who says that it is a property of the Sun to be 'the brightest star that moves above the earth' has employed in the property something of a kind which is comprehensible only by sensation, namely 'moving above the earth' and so the property of the Sun would not have been correctly assigned, for it will not be manifest when the Sun sets, whether it is still moving above the earth, because sensation then fails us. (Derrida 1982: 250)

This way of identifying the Sun supposedly fails because it lacks generality as we cannot see how bright the Sun is at night. But before we accept this as a valid criticism, it is worth noting that there actually was a 'he' who said this. Though neither Aristotle nor Derrida indicates the origin of the example, it turns out that it was invented by Socrates in his dialogue with Theatetus. Their entire dialogue is concerned with what it is to know anything. It is highly relevant to our overall concerns in this book because even their first exchanges hint that the problem of knowledge surfaces in the difficulty of telling things apart. The person who introduces Theatetus to Socrates remarks that he may see a resemblance between them because they both have snub noses. Toward the end, Socrates returns to this theme, noting that 'right opinion implies the perception of differences' (Plato 1949: ll.209, 83) and therefore to correctly identify either him or Theatetus, they would need to be able to differentiate them. Therefore, they would need to do more than just appreciate what they have in common, i.e. a type of nose.

More to the point, the whole dialogue attempts to teach Theatetus precisely by trying to get him not to confuse things that he already has some understanding of. First, he needs to learn that there is a difference between perception and knowledge. Then, that there is a difference between opinion and knowledge. Then, that there is even a difference between *right* opinion and knowledge. Also, throughout, he is probably learning that there can be a difference between another two things he begins by equating: wisdom and knowledge. If there is this real problem differentiating things, which Theatetus's various confusions certainly indicate there is, it makes us wonder if there is any way out of the confusion. What Socrates finally suggests, almost at the end of the dialogue, is finding 'the mark or sign of difference which distinguishes the thing in question from all others' (Plato 1949: ll.208, 81).

On the one hand this does seem right and even exciting as a potential solution to their problem. Surely if one could find that one thing that clearly differentiates it from everything it could well be confused with, one would be very unlikely to ever confuse it with those things again. And even if that one thing was hard to detect and so confusion remained a possibility, at least one would know, whenever possible confusion arose, what to look out for. On the other hand, it seems a daunting, even perhaps a sometimes impossible task to find such a thing, the distinguishing mark. Having heard Socrates' suggestion, Theatetus asks: 'Can you give me any example of such a definition?' (Plato 1949: ll.208, 81). The fact that he asks for *any* example suggests both that, while he senses that to be able to manage to find such a thing would be *extremely* helpful, he also finds it hard to believe any such thing could ever actually be found. It is at this point that Socrates introduces the example that Aristotle finds so unsatisfactory: 'As for example in the case of the Sun I think you would be contented with the statement that the Sun is the brightest of the heavenly bodies which revolve around the earth.' Theatetus responds: 'certainly' (ll.208, 82).

It is probably not right to conclude that Aristotle, in making the criticism with which we began this chapter, was a more perspicuous student than Theatetus. It is more that, unlike Aristotle, Theatetus' certainty indicates that he had a better understanding of what there was a need for: not a general definition listing every imaginable property of the Sun but a way that would help us differentiate the Sun from things we could possibly confuse it with. It is surely right that if we set out to find the Sun, looking for the brightest object in the heavens would be a satisfactory method of minimizing the likely sources of confusion.

Of course, we would expect the method of identifying the differentiating mark to be used for more significant matters than helping someone not to confuse the Sun with other heavenly bodies. One example is how Socrates is portrayed as teaching two generals, Laches and Nicias, in the early Platonic dialogue, *Laches*. In Laches' engagement with Socrates he first defines courage as a man who 'is willing to remain at his post and to defend himself against the enemy without running away' (Plato 1973: 190e, 31). Socrates objects that this neglects 'the one who fights with the enemy, not holding his ground' (191a, 32). We can anticipate (as later exchanges in the dialogue confirm) that Laches' specific problem is that he is confusing courage with rashness. That is, while he has the very admirable inclination to be courageous, he is prone to mix it up with something else, rashness, to which it does, admittedly, bear a strong resemblance. What is stimulating about how Socrates proceeds is that Socrates can be read as finding a distinguishing mark that could indeed help Laches to tell the difference between these two things. What he suggests to Laches is that surely he would not want to do anything that 'is accompanied by folly' (192c, 34). Just as anyone who is trying to find the Sun can be safely advised to look for the brightest star in the sky, anyone prone to confuse courage with rashness is well advised to avoid actions that smack of folly. In other words and phrased as a message to Laches: 'If you are at least careful not to do anything that seems clearly foolish, you will be much less likely to make the particular mistake that you are prone to, namely being merely rash when you are trying to be courageous.'

Nicias' starting point in his engagement with Socrates is very different. What he initially insists on is that 'if a man is really courageous, it is clear that he is wise' (Plato 1973: 194d, 38). Under questioning from Socrates, it soon becomes apparent that what he means by wisdom is really a totally risk-free life, even to the point that he relies on seers for all his major decisions, such as whether to launch an attack. It seems he too is confusing two things, in his case being wise with never risking anything and never undertaking an action while being unsure of the result. We need to consider if there is any one thing that would enable him to stop confusing wisdom with leading *such* a risk-adverse life. If what would help Laches is to remember not to be foolish, while *that* could never be Nicias' problem, it would greatly help him to remember the danger of being downright cowardly. This mnemonic would enable him to stop confusing wisdom with the attempt to abolish all risk.

Often, particularly in the dialogues that are supposedly inconclusive, i.e. dialogues that never arrive at a 'positive' definition, Plato includes hints that the end is not really unsatisfactory because the characters have been taught what they needed to learn. Such can be seen to be the case with both Laches and Nicias. The dialogue began with a third person, Lysimachos, asking Laches, Nicias, and Socrates for advice on how to educate his sons. At the end, Laches says he would let Socrates teach his own sons: '*If* my boys were the same age' (Plato 1973: 200c, 48, emphasis added). As this is an unusually careful sort of endorsement to come from someone like him, we can say he may well, as he needs to, be becoming less prone to overhasty and therefore foolish (but seemingly courageous) decisions. Nicias, at the start, had reported that he once asked Socrates for a music teacher for his son. At the end, he reveals that really this was his obtuse way of trying to get Socrates himself as his son's teacher without directly asking him. As he tells us now: 'In fact I would gladly entrust Niceratus to him, if he is willing. But whenever I bring up the subject in any way, he always recommends other people to me but is unwilling to take on the job himself' (200d, 48).

Instead of the cowardly (but apparently wise) strategy of beating around the bush, the point is that he has finally become brave enough to risk an open question to which he may or may not get the answer he wants.

In his *Ethics*, Aristotle, too, offers guidance on what constitutes virtuous behavior, including being courageous. In fact, courage is the first virtue he discusses and, clearly influenced by Plato's analysis of it, some of what he says sounds quite similar to what is developed in the *Laches*. Aristotle writes: 'The man who shuns and fears everything and stands up to nothing becomes a coward, the man who is afraid of nothing at all, but marches up to every danger, becomes foolhardy' (Aristotle 1976: 1104a11, 94).

Though some awareness of where both a Nicias and a Laches are going wrong does seem present here, what is missing is a clear recognition of the *good* things that people like these are attempting to achieve. There is no sense either of the admirable effort, however misguided, of those who end up being prone to cowardice to act wisely, or the equally admirable but also equally misguided effort of those who tend to commit foolhardy actions to act courageously.

Because of this failure to appreciate what is admirable about both these sorts of persons' starting points, Aristotle comes across as just rebuking persons for pursuing two clearly undesirable alternatives (being a coward and being a fool) rather than helping them to rectify their understandable mistakes. What form can moral guidance take when there is this lack of appreciation of the *specific* confusions (on the one hand confusing wisdom with wishing to completely avoid risk, on the other hand confusing courage with a willingness to do things no matter how rash they might appear) that are misleading such people? Instead of being able to develop a particular suggestion for each of their problems, i.e. in the first case be careful not to lapse into actions that are clearly cowardly, in the second, be careful to avoid a course of action that only a fool would be likely to embark on, one ends up offering a rule that supposedly covers everyone. The upshot, for Aristotle, is the (we say undeservedly) famous doctrine of the mean: 'It is possible [...] to feel fear, confidence, desire, anger, pity, and pleasure generally, too much or too little, and both of these are wrong' (Aristotle 1976: 1107a1, 101).

Because there is no understanding of the specific confusions that are at work here, instead of specific suggestions as to what various types need to learn, we get a proposed recipe that can, if followed, supposedly make anyone virtuous. But apart from the obvious difficulty in following a recipe that tells us only not to use either a lot or a little of any of the ingredients, there is the question of why anyone would ever want to follow it. As this dilemma applies to courage, why should a Nicias be inclined to listen to someone who claims he is wrong to have as much fear as he does when first, who is to say that the would-be wise person is actually experiencing great fear? And second, even if he is, why is he likely to be convinced that is a disgrace rather than a sign of how wise he is? Similarly, why should a Laches pay any attention to someone who is suggesting he has too little fear when, first, perhaps he has quite a lot of fear that he is proudly controlling? And second, when even if he does not have much fear, he could be seeing his relative lack of fear as a sign of how courageous he is?

The way Plato has Socrates treat Glaucon, the character in *The Republic* who we already saw complaining that he does not wish to live in a city of pigs, provides a much more complex example of teaching by helping someone differentiate two things he is confusing. Already in Book I, before Glaucon has entered the scene in a substantial way, Socrates has tried to stop another character, Polemarchos, from confusing two things, in his case justice with vengeance. The method is to suggest that as justice must be something good, it should not be used, as is vengeance (by how it treats enemies) to harm anyone. But, as Book II begins, Glaucon asks how good justice can actually be since it is actually *injustice* that potentially gives all sorts of good things. He says look at all the pleasurable things an unjust person can do: get whatever he wants, seduce other people's wives, become a tyrant and therefore take possession of the wealth of entire cities. On the other hand, apart from a good reputation (with even that not being at all certain as the just can seem unjust) is not justice simply painful deprivation of personal pleasures? (Plato 1974: ll.354d–62c, 102–8).

The question that becomes relevant once one sees Glaucon's starting point is how to teach him. We will discover that besides trying to depict what justice is, Socrates simultaneously orients to Glaucon's specific needs by understanding that he, like Laches and Nicias, is suffering from a specific confusion. The reason he is unable to see how justice is better than injustice is because he is confusing the good with pleasure.

But managing to remove this confusion, especially if it is to be done in a way helpful to Glaucon who, as we have already seen, does have quite a developed and legitimate interest in pleasure, is no easy task. We shall examine some of Socrates' key moves; in effect his strategy as a teacher. The first one occurs when he is talking to another character, Adeimantos. We can assume that Glaucon is listening. Socrates asks: 'Justice can be a characteristic of an individual or of a community, can it not?' (Plato 1974: 368e, 117).

Adeimantos agrees. We can say that, whereas Glaucon began by wondering how justice can be a good if it does not give him personally pleasure, Socrates is suggesting that if justice is our topic, we will need to understand that we might need to notice one property of what is good that can differentiate it from how we normally think of pleasure, namely it—what is good—can apply to a collective as well as to an individual.

It is actually when he has learned this lesson that Glaucon objects that all that Socrates has so far produced is fare for a city of pigs. He is then still thinking of what could make justice good as equivalent to what could make it pleasurable but now at least with the understanding that it would be a whole collective, and not just an individual, that would enjoy the various pleasures. As we saw in the previous chapter, Socrates does not object to trying to analyze what justice would be in the sort of (pleasurable) city Glaucon craves but he does say: 'With our new luxuries we shall need doctors too, far more than we did before.' Glaucon agrees: 'We certainly shall' (Plato 1973: 373d, 123).

In terms of our theme that what Glaucon needs to learn is not to confuse the good with pleasure, we can say that now, besides learning that, compared to pleasure, what is good is more a notion that applies to a collective as well as an individual, he is also learning that another difference between the good and pleasure is that not all pleasures are good for the obvious reason that some pleasures are really pretty sure to make you sick.

There follows a long discussion, during which Glaucon is silent, of various aspects of the education necessary for the rulers in what would be a just city. When Socrates says that having discussed many other aspects of their education, they had better say a little about what would constitute a suitable musical education as well, even he seems to want to cut the discussion short. But here Glaucon re-enters, insisting they do go into this subject in detail. He also unwittingly reveals he knows quite a lot about music, much more than Socrates. Music being a form of pleasure, his attachment to it fits with the sense that he is someone strongly committed to extracting pleasure from life. Most commentators have not paid much attention to this section and, when they have, treat Socrates as merely continuing with his now notorious insistence on excluding by censorship most forms of art as bad for the rulers' education.

However, unlike how he deals with literature, Socrates does not exactly argue that some forms of music should be excluded, irrespective of how enjoyable he thinks they are. He tries instead to depict the *ugliness* of the music he thinks should be rejected. For example, both saccharine and bombastic music are rejected because they are repulsive to persons of refined taste. We can say that Glaucon is being shown another way in which what is good and what is pleasurable can be differentiated. It is not just that some pleasures are not healthy. Some are better and some are worse on aesthetic grounds. Therefore, at least those with taste should see that the good and at least some concepts of pleasure are not the same idea. And, in this case, seeing how good a thing is, aesthetically, can actually affect how much pleasure a person with the kind of developed interest in pleasure Glaucon has can even derive from the thing.

Next Socrates proceeds, still in conversation with Glaucon, to use a similar argument to show how anyone aspiring to be a leader in their emerging city would need to keep reasonably fit by some exercise and not eating things like 'attic confectionary' (Plato 1973: 1.404d, 167). He portrays a person who would not act as he is suggesting as weak, unattractive, and given to flatulence and catarrh. We say Glaucon is again being helped to see that certain forms of pleasure should not be confused with what is good, now not just if one wants to stay healthy but also if one wants to be at least minimally attractive to others.

Glaucon's next major intervention occurs in Book IV when, having completed to his satisfaction a description of the imaginary city that could be just, Socrates wonders where, exactly, justice could be found in it. He says that if their city is perfect, it will 'obviously have the qualities of wisdom, courage, discipline and justice' (Plato 1973: 1.427d, 197). Having located both wisdom and courage, Socrates says: 'Well, we are left with two qualities to look for in our state, self-discipline and the real object of our whole inquiry, justice [...] I wonder if we could find justice without having to bother further about self-discipline.' Glaucon replies: 'Personally [...] I shouldn't want to find it if it meant we were to give up looking for self-discipline. What I should like you to do is to look for self-discipline first' (Plato 1974: 430d, 201).

What is worth noting is that the same person who was unwilling to look for justice if it were going to deprive him and his city of luxury now has an active desire to look for self-discipline. As self-discipline would clearly only appear worth pursuing—a good—to someone who believed that there were other goods than the unimpeded search for pleasure, we can say that Glaucon is continuing to take on board the lesson that what can be good and what is pleasurable are distinct notions.

As they develop it, what self-discipline is is when all the parts of the city or all the parts of a person are in agreement on letting the best part make the decisions. Socrates says this best part, whether of a city or of a person, is the part that has a sense of what is wise. Now they do get to the question of justice. Justice is said also to concern coordination among all the parts, whether of a city or a person. Justice is when *all* the parts do what they are best at or, as Socrates puts it, when they all mind their own business.

It is certainly possible, with the hindsight our contemporary position provides, to find fault with this notion. It does not seem to have much sense of what, for much of recent history, has been the thrust of the idea of justice: rectifying inequality. But if we recall that Glaucon wanted an account of how justice could be something good, it can be suggested that all the parts doing what they are best at does make justice seem something that would be good, unlike for example, if all justice were was vengeance. However, if this version of justice is meant as Socrates' last word as to what the good is, a new problem surfaces for Glaucon. While he might be permanently cured of confusing the good with pleasure, particularly since control by the wise part, whether of a person or a city, means that individual and group desires are definitely not in control, *so* different do what is good and what is pleasurable now seem that he could certainly be forgiven for thinking that, if he had to choose, he might, in spite of all he has learned about the limits of certain types of pleasure, opt for pleasure after all—perhaps in more moderate form—over the good.

But what is the good? It is fair to say that, at this point, we must think that the good is to be identified with the presence of justice so long as it coexists, as it inevitably would in Socrates' conception of it, with the presence of the other virtues as well: wisdom, temperance, and courage. This is clearly what Socrates' other main interlocutor, Adeimantos, thinks, as witness his surprise when, in Book VI, Socrates says that there is something 'higher' than justice and the rest and unless he grasps it 'he will never finally reach the highest form of knowledge' (Plato 1974: 504d, 302).

It is only a slight caricature to say that Adeimantos' reaction is the disappointment of being told that he has not learned enough already. It is roughly here that Glaucon makes another interruption, this time literally begging Socrates to say at least something about this highest thing, the good. Why would Glaucon be so actively motivated to hear about what is higher than justice? We would suggest that there are good reasons why he is both not as surprised as Adeimantos to hear there is such a thing and eager to hear what it might be. In that he had that initial worry that, unless there could be pleasure gathered from justice, it is not clear why we should be committed to it, we can say that Glaucon had, on his own, sensed that there might be something 'higher' than justice, i.e. a prior demand that it must satisfy. His problem is that he identifies this prior necessity with pleasure.

We have suggested that what he has been gradually learning ever since is that pleasure may be a more problematic category than he was able to imagine at the start. We suggest now that his eagerness to hear what might be higher than justice stems from a hope that, if this higher thing could somehow not rule out the more refined version of what could be pleasurable that he is starting to discover, then at least some forms of pleasure seeking and justice seeking are not incompatible after all. But can such compatibility be established?

As Socrates begins to discuss this highest thing, the form of the good, he re-emphasizes that it is not knowledge or pleasure or justice. While it is none of these things, it is what 'things which are just and so on derive their usefulness and value from' (Plato 1974: 505a, 303).

We begin to suspect it is a strange kind of thing or maybe not a specific *thing* at all. What happens next will be doubly interesting to us. First, we get a sense of what the good is that, arguably, will enable Glaucon never to again confuse it with pleasure while also showing him how he need not give up on pleasure if he orients to what is good. But the other interest for us is that when Socrates tries to depict what the good is, he does not offer a conventional definition. Instead, he offers a metaphor.

He says the good resembles the Sun. It is like the Sun because the good does in the realm of ideas such as justice, what the Sun does for material objects. As the Sun supplies the light that lets us see clearly things like trees, the good supplies the light that lets us see clearly matters such as what justice is (Plato 1974: 508b, 308). While most commentators, actually starting with Aristotle, have either been puzzled by the metaphor, objected to it, or both,[1] we can suggest that it works as a fitting way to visualize Socrates' own method of analysis as we have already seen it displayed in *The Republic*. That is, in order to arrive at his conclusions, especially about justice, he has tried to attain clarity by letting his conclusions about the notion be oriented by his sense of what could be good about it. The most obvious example is that it is only by insisting, in Book I, that justice, if seen clearly, must be something good that he was stimulated to dismiss Polemarchos' belief that justice could be vengeance. If justice did not need to be something good, there is no reason why it should not be vengeance. Similarly, his method for realizing that he must discuss not just individual justice but also justice in the city, stemmed from his sense that justice had to be a good thing and for justice to be a good thing, it must be good for more than just individuals. Or, as suggested above, even if we moderns cannot be satisfied with Socrates' final definition of justice as all the parts doing what they do best, we cannot deny that this way of defining it could stem from a need to see what could be good about it.

So it makes sense that Socrates thinks the Sun is what the good is like (both shed light, albeit on different sorts of things) but how will this way of thinking about it help Glaucon? First, if he understands that the good is no one thing but what can enable him to see more clearly various things, there is no way he will be likely to continue confusing it with pleasure. But also, and crucially, if this is what the good is like, it would not only be able to enable us to see justice more clearly. It would also help us to see other things more clearly too. One of these other things it could help us have a better grasp of would be the nature of (including the varieties of) pleasure. This would take the form of helping us to see which forms of pleasure would be most worth pursuing because of how good (or at least not bad) they are. Though not all would be, clearly many forms of pleasure, when seen in the light of how good they are, would be compatible with justice.

And it can also be noted that, while the explicit depiction of what the good is like has only just been made, it is a formulation of what has come before. For just as Socrates has been using the method he is now becoming explicit about throughout in how he analyzes justice, he has also been using it in how he analyzes pleasure. The clearer version of pleasure that he has been offering Glaucon, according to which some pleasures were seen as unhealthy, others as too individual, and still others as downright ugly, was only possible because he was letting his sense of what is good shed light on how he (and Glaucon) should see pleasure.

Like his analysis of courage, Aristotle's analysis of pleasure is clearly influenced by Plato and does sound similar. Aristotle writes:

> Since all knowledge and every pursuit aims at some good [...] what is the highest of all practical goods? Well, so far as the name goes it is happiness [...] but when it comes to saying in what happiness consists, opinions differ, and the account given by the generality of mankind is not at all like that of the wise. The former take it to be something obvious and familiar, like pleasure. (Aristotle 1976: 1095a7, 66)

The wise, like Plato's wise, will be those who realize that pleasure is not the good. Or again, in a passage that is surprising in the light of the fact that Nussbaum, the Aristotelian, was so critical of the fact that *Plato* compared us to cattle:

> To judge by their lives, the masses and the most vulgar seem—not unreasonably—to believe the good or happiness is pleasure. Accordingly they ask nothing better than the life of enjoyment [...] The utter servility of the masses comes out in their preference for a *bovine* existence. (Aristotle 1976: 1095b14, 68, emphasis added)

So Aristotle, too, wants to convince us that the good is not pleasure. But Plato said the reason we tend to think pleasure is the good is because we do not know what the good is like. Aristotle, on the other hand, is saying that there is no confusion about what the good is. The good is clear. It is, both the wise and 'the vulgar' agree, happiness.

But then why, in this account, is pleasure not the good since surely it is not just the vulgar masses who get happiness from pleasures? What exactly is wrong with just pursuing pleasure? His idea is to attempt to articulate the proper relationship to pleasure in the same way that he tried to articulate the proper relationship to courage. Just as we should not have either too much or too little fear: 'In the field of Pleasures and Pains [...] the mean is Temperance, the excess Licentiousness; cases of defective response to pleasure scarcely occur, and therefore people of this sort [...] have no name to describe them, but let us class them as Insensible' (Aristotle 1976: 1107a28, 103).

Deprived of Plato's method of reflecting on the goodness of things in order to gain a clearer view of them, Aristotle has no way to identify pleasures that, on reflection, we come to see as bad; as not worth our while. Therefore he cannot see that there would be at least some and possibly many pleasures that really there cannot be too little of. At the same time, he also cannot identify pleasures that, on reflection, seem so good that, perhaps short of being obsessed with them, really there is no reason why we should not allow ourselves as much as we want.

Irrespective of its detrimental effect on our ability to learn what pleasures to avoid and which to pursue, treating happiness as the good also leads to an additional unfortunate result. Aristotle is unable to recognize that there are collective goods and that there can be decisions that can be good because of what they accomplish for a collective. This means there can sometimes be good decisions that, even if they accept them willingly, some individuals will not be particularly happy about because they do not benefit from them personally. For example, many just decisions would have this property.

While Aristotle's approach does seem to be making him less effective as a teacher because his ideas just tell us what to think from scratch rather than help us out of our own confusions and, also, because his ideas are much too vague, this is not to say that there are not consequences that he would find it extremely difficult to welcome were he to change course. Unlike the idea that the good is like the Sun, his idea that the good is happiness has the form of a factual claim. It therefore seems serviceable as a major premise.[2] The idea that among the things that can lead to this happiness are not too much or too little fear and not too much or too little pleasure also has the form of a factual claim. It seems serviceable as a minor premise. Taken together they amount to a syllogism that makes Aristotle's judgment that we should be (according to his definitions of them) courageous and temperate, seem merely a logical deduction. He could not move to another way of teaching without taking the radical step of abandoning his preferred mode of reasoning. He would also have to take the additional radical step of revising his version of the person in need of teaching since, as was argued in the previous chapter, the mistakes such a person is likely to be making that are the province of the teacher, i.e. mistakes of similarity and difference, are material for comedy, not tragedy.

Besides clarifying the teacher's task, it can be suggested that this chapter simultaneously clarifies a feature of the method of comparison. While the method does require differentiating phenomena, it does *not* require locating any and all differences between things. The task is just to locate differences that can help with confusions, locating, then, distinguishing marks such as the ones Socrates finds.

Notes

1   Aristotle 1976: 1096a19, 69–71. See also Heidegger 1961: 89–90 and Rosen 1969: 140–97.
2   Hence Macintyre's use of this idea in Chapter 5.

Chapter 10

Oriented Action

While our starting point and focus so far in this book have been on metaphors as an alternative to syllogisms, the need for good judgment and how metaphoric reasoning can help one achieve it will be better understood if it can be seen as not merely a response to the failure of syllogisms. In this chapter, we look at how this need can also be understood as a way of overcoming certain self-confessed limitations in the way that, in the works of Max Weber, the whole realm of social action has been analyzed and critiqued.[1] Weber quotes Tolstoi's damning critique of science: 'Science is meaningless because it gives no answer to our question, the only question important for us. "What shall we do and how shall we live"' (Weber 1947a: 143).

But, without disagreeing with Tolstoi, Weber hints that his own 'science' might not be exactly useless in this regard:

> That science does not give an answer to this is indisputable. The only question that remains is the sense in which science gives 'no' answer, and whether or not science might yet be of some use to the one who puts the question correctly. (Weber 1947a: 143)

Undoubtedly what Weber believes could be of 'some use' here is his own consideration of the possible answers to the question of 'what shall we do.' Weber, then, will have advice about developing judgment. His relevant ideas can be extracted from his classification of 'the types of social action' (Weber 1947b: 115–8).

Weber begins by excluding, as not even social, behavior that has no discernible orientation, behavior that precisely because it lacks any such orientation, can only seem senseless, unintelligible. Even pointing to what should be excluded is of 'some use' for an interest in deciding what to do because, while examples of such behavior certainly exist (think of gibberish and/or some forms of random mass murder), behaving senselessly cannot be the answer to Tolstoi's question.

But there are also two types of admittedly *social* action, forms of action that Weber can locate an orientation for and that, therefore, he finds intelligible but that he cannot endorse as of use in solving the problem of judging what we should do.[2] These types are acting 'in terms of affectual orientation, especially emotional, determined by the specific affects and states of feeling of the actor' (Weber 1947b: 115). Or, acting in ways that are 'traditionally oriented, through the habituation of long practice' (115). Weber depicts what is problematic about traditionally oriented behavior as follows:

> Strictly traditional behavior [...] lies very close to the borderline of what can justifiably be called meaningfully oriented action, and indeed often on the other side. For it is very often a matter of almost automatic reaction to habitual stimuli which guide behavior in a course that has been repeatedly followed. (Weber 1947b: 116)

In our terms, we can say that to act on such grounds is not to be exercising good or, for that matter, even bad judgment since an accurate version of such action is that, due to its automatic character, one cannot be said to be judging at all. It is unlikely that such a procedure could lead to adequate answers in important decisions as to what to do.

Weber also sees affectual behavior as far less than ideal because not fully oriented: 'Purely affectual behavior also stands on the borderline of what can be considered "meaningfully" oriented and often it, too, goes over the line' (Weber 1947b: 116).

The way this form of behavior tends to be unoriented is not that one acts too automatically. Instead, what concerns Weber is that 'it may, for instance consist in an uncontrolled reaction to some exceptional stimulus' (Weber 1947b: 116).

As this would apply to our interest, it is a truism that affectual factors such as current emotion or mood can easily have a detrimental effect on the faculty of judgment.

There are two other possible modes of orientation that Weber allows. One can be guided by a

> rational orientation to a system of discrete individual ends, that is, through expectations as to the behavior of objects in the external situation and of other human individuals, making use of these expectations as 'conditions' or 'means' for the successful attainment of the actor's own rationally chosen ends. (Weber 1947b: 115)

Weber further explains what he has in mind by this sort of orientation. It is when

> the end, means, and the secondary results are all rationally taken into account and weighed. This involves rational consideration of alternative means to the end, of the relation of the end to other prospective results of employment of any given means, and finally of the relative importance of different possible ends. (Weber 1947b: 117)

While Weber gives no specific cases at this point, his translator, Talcott Parsons, suggests that a good example of the kind of end that one could orient to rationally in this way would be money (Weber 1947b: 115, footnote). Thus, one could decide, after weighing various ends, that the end that is most important to one is not, say, helping people, but making a lot of money. Reaching this conclusion could then help a great deal in judging what means, e.g. surely not becoming a school teacher, can be expected to aid one in attaining this end.

But Weber, somewhat surprisingly, also offers another way of orienting that he also considers rational. One can have a 'rational orientation to an absolute value; involving a conscious belief in the absolute value of some ethical, aesthetic, religious, or other form of behaviour, entirely for its own sake and independently of any prospects of external success' (Weber 1947b: 115).

In this case, Weber himself does offer several examples:

> Examples of pure rational orientation to absolute values would be the action of persons who, regardless of possible cost to themselves, act to put into practice their conviction of what seems to them to be required by duty, honour, the pursuit of beauty, a religious call, personal loyalty, or the importance of some 'cause' no matter in what it consists. (Weber 1947b: 116)

How could identifying these two possible ways of orienting be relevant to helping us with Tolstoi's question? First, Weber probably thinks that only those who are oriented in either of these two ways have any realistic hope of making good judgments about what to do with their lives. Thus, he explicitly says of his first version of rational action that 'determination of action, either in affectual or traditional terms, is [...] incompatible with this type' (Weber 1947b: 117). However, there also is a much more specific way in which he believes his own approach can be of 'some use.' He writes: 'The primary task of a useful teacher is to teach his students to recognize "inconvenient" facts' (Weber 1947a: 147).

What he means becomes clear if we examine his own writing, which is to say what *he* is trying to teach us. It is only a slight exaggeration to say most of it consists of a set of inconvenient facts. For example, concerning the prospects for a career as a university teacher in the Germany of his times, he writes: 'Academic life is a mad hazard. If the young scholar asks for my advice [...] the responsibility of encouraging him can hardly be borne. If he is a Jew, of course one says lasciate ogni speranza'[3] (Weber 1947a: 134).

The usefulness of this is obvious. Imagine one of the possible ends that someone is weighing is a career as a university teacher. If she happens to be Jewish, thanks to the fact Weber has just alerted her to, she would know that the conditions and means are such that what would be rational is to choose another end.

The inconvenient facts can also be much less obvious. For example, in his analysis of politics, he writes: 'He who seeks the salvation of the soul, of his own and of others, should not seek it along the avenue of politics, for the quite different tasks of politics can only be solved by violence' (Weber 1947c: 126).

The violence of politics has the status of another inconvenient fact. Teaching this fact has the simultaneous use of advising those whose end is salvation that they should not rationally expect politics to be the means to that end and advising those who are inclined to chose politics as their end, both that they should not rationally expect to be saving anyone's soul and that, whether they like it or not, they will sometimes have to advocate violence.

Having acknowledged the potential usefulness of Weber's method, it must be noted that he only claims that his work is of *some* use. There are at least two ways in which the limits of his method can be seen. First, it can be suggested that it is possible, even probable, that a person could recognize one or, indeed, many inconvenient facts without that being a factor sufficient to make them likely to change their mind. A case in point is Weber himself. He is careful to note that his method can lead even him to be confronted by inconvenient facts: 'And for every […] opinion there are facts that are extremely inconvenient, for my own opinion no less than for others' (Weber 1947a: 147).

What is telling is that the wording suggests that, as inconvenient as these facts are, they have more made him feel uncomfortable about his opinion than caused him to radically revise his beliefs.

An example confirms the suspicion that even very inconvenient facts may have minimal impact on decisions. He mentions a fact about university life that applies even to those, like Weber, who do not happen to be Jewish: 'Do you in all conscience believe you can stand seeing mediocrity after mediocrity year after year climb beyond you, without becoming embittered and without coming to grief?' (Weber 1947a: 134). As unpalatable as this fact about the nature of promotions no doubt is to him, it is clear it has not caused him to abandon academia.

A second problem is that inconvenient facts would seem to impact only on his first type of rationality. This is because it is hard to see how facts that by and large pertain to whether it will actually be possible to realize wished for ends by a particular course of action, can be brought to bear when one is so absolutely committed to a value that one does not care about 'prospects of external success' (Weber 1947b: 115) or that one will act 'regardless of possible cost to themselves' (116). As some confirmation, it is worth seeing how little use Weber's method is in evaluating a typical absolute value. He writes:

> What man will take upon himself the attempt to 'refute scientifically' the ethic of the Sermon on the Mount? For instance, the sentence, 'resist no evil,' or the image of turning the other cheek? And yet it is clear, in mundane perspective, that this is an ethic of undignified conduct; one has to choose between the religious dignity which this ethic confers and the dignity of manly conduct which preaches something quite different; 'resist evil—lest you be co-responsible for an overpowering evil.' According to our ultimate standpoint, the one is the devil and the other the God, and the individual has to decide which is God for him and which is the devil. (Weber 1947a: 148)

While it would not be right to conclude that he has nothing to say about this ethic, it is clear that instead of inconvenient facts all he can offer is a contrasting ethic, as he says another 'perspective.' As the last sentence indicates, he is so powerless to help us choose between these two ethics that he cannot even advise us as to which would amount to the way of the devil.

It can be concluded that Weber is right that his method is of only limited use. In the case of the first type of rationality, he can only help us understand whether a goal is achievable and, if it is, what inconvenient means we will need to accept if we are going to manage to attain it. No more direct assessments of the demerits or, for that matter, the merits of the goal are possible. In the case of the second type of rationality, as his own formulation of the sort of values he has in mind as 'absolute' or 'ultimate' suggests, there is seemingly nothing he can offer that can either shake, affirm, or even refine these values.

Our argument is that, for both Weber's types of rationality, metaphoric reasoning can be of use in helping us to overcome the limits that Weber's method has imposed. For example, arriving with Dante's help at a sense of what flattery is like, with another author's help at a sense of what being a housewife is like, or with Plato's help at what the life of a businessman is like, are ways of finding hard to deny problems with these activities that can stand even though we can concede that these remain possible achievements and that whatever inconvenient facts we might be able to cite might well not be sufficient to warn us off these ways of life.

I would also argue that even what Weber would consider absolute values can be evaluated with the aid of appropriate metaphors. Two examples may suffice, the first invented, the second drawn from a theorist's intervention in a current controversy. Imagine that one has some embarrassing inside information about a communal matter that really is no business of outsiders. It is certainly possible that someone in the community who has a Weber-style absolute commitment to honesty might feel it is his duty to reveal the information to all comers. It can be suggested that remarking to this person that he is acting *like* a reporter might well stimulate him to reassess the merits of his supposedly absolute value.

The second example is the way a metaphor produced by Ronald Dworkin manages a compelling critique of another decision seemingly made necessary by someone's ultimate value. At the time Dworkin is writing, it is unclear whether the US Supreme Court will rule Obama's health care reforms unconstitutional. Because the Court contains five resolutely conservative justices it looks likely that Obama will lose the case. In Weber's terms, this would be the inevitable consequence of them, rationally, following their ultimate values. However, Dworkin develops a form of reasoning that could work with one of the judges, the only one Dworkin sees as at all open to a form (to be specified) of reason. Addressing this one justice, Anthony Kennedy, he writes:

> If the Court does declare the act unconstitutional, it would have ruled that Congress lacks the power to adopt what it thought the most effective, efficient, fair, and politically workable remedy [...] for the sole reason that in the Court's opinion our Constitution is a strict and arbitrary document that denies our national legislature the power to enact the only possible national program. If that opinion were right, we would have to accept that our eighteenth-century Constitution is not the enduring marvel of statesmanship we suppose but an anachronistic, crippling burden we cannot escape, a *straightjacket* that makes it impossible for us to achieve a just national society. (Dworkin 2012: 4, emphasis added)

It is important that we reiterate that this argument is directed toward a conservative, that is to someone who is committed to, i.e. whose ultimate value demands, a strict, even perhaps a near literal interpretation of the Constitution. The point is that Dworkin has found a way to do what Weber considers impossible, not merely contrast this value with another value, e.g. a liberal one, but judge the value in question from, as it were, within. He is stimulating Judge Kennedy to rethink what he ought to do by helping him to appreciate what his own values would be *like*, i.e. a straightjacket, if he interprets the document that he rightly considers marvelous in an excessively strict and arbitrary way. If he can see that *his own* values do not need to be *like* a straightjacket, he has a way of seeing how, without at all needing to abandon his absolute, namely that the Constitution is an enduring marvel, it is still not his duty to find the health care reforms unconstitutional.[4]

Clearly, apt metaphors such as the ones just cited can be just as inconvenient if not more so than Weber's facts. They can force one to rethink one's goals and even the meaning of one's ultimate values. Admittedly, metaphors, even the most apt ones, lack various seemingly attractive features of facts. For example, they cannot sustain the air of neutrality that many factual statements have and they are never as incontestable as statements of fact can be.[5] But their power to judge even acts that, to all appearances, are rational means that we would be unwise to be dismissive of them on these or other grounds.

By insisting that his method will limit itself to citing facts, Weber is clearly aligning himself with those such as Aristotle and Popper who believe that they have no need to utilize aesthetic techniques. However, instead of the straightforwardly empiricist strategy of claiming to merely observe facts, we have seen that, in order to make his method useful in helping us to arrive at judgments, he has had to narrow his focus to *inconvenient* facts.

While we have already suggested that listing inconvenient facts does not offer as much help at arriving at judgments as developing metaphors does, a further question can now be considered. How accurate is Weber's self-assessment that he limits himself in this way? Like politics and academia as a whole, Weber's specific field, what he calls science, also has an inconvenient fact. Weber writes that 'the technique of mastering life which rests upon science has been celebrated as the way to happiness' (Weber 1947a: 143).

The inconvenient fact is that, certainly in Weber's opinion, it cannot achieve this end. But how is this fact not *so* inconvenient that he could advise no rational person to undertake a career in science? If he sticks to his method, he will need to find at least some facts that could make it rational *not* to abandon science even if it can no longer be celebrated in this way. Does he manage to do so? He writes: 'After Nietzsche's devastating criticism of those "last men" who "invented happiness," [...] Who believes in this?—aside from a few big children in university chairs or editorial offices' (Weber 1947a: 143).

Clearly, Weber is here doing what he can to help us judge these people. In terms of the question of whether his method is equal to this task, one possibly inconvenient fact that he is able to observe is that there are only 'a few' of these people left. It can, of course, be inconvenient, should we be tempted to follow this route, to have to face the fact that we would be in a tiny minority. In this way, the more limited type of science that Weber advocates could begin to seem somewhat more attractive. However, it is questionable whether such a fact would be all that helpful in judging one way or the other. After all, the very person whose criticism of overly optimistic scientists Weber cites is well known for inventing a character, Zarathustra, whose teaching Nietzsche recommends even though what it proclaims is most certainly a minority view.

Weber himself can be seen to realize that he has not yet offered sufficient help in deciding whether it might be rational to become a scientist in spite of the field's limitations, in that he proceeds to offer another characterization of those who he thinks have an illusory and exaggerated view of science's potential. He says they are 'big children.' On the one hand, if this amounts to a fact about them, he would surely have managed to have observed an inconvenient fact that would put most, if not all, rational people off. Who would want to be a big child? And, as seems justifiable if scientists with *this* belief are childish, this enables Weber to observe what appears to be a very *convenient* fact about scientists like him who have a more modest view of what their field can accomplish. He says that they 'bear the fate of the times like a man' (Weber 1947a: 155).

However, even if Weber had not used the word 'like' here, it takes only a moment's reflection to realize that, however inconvenient the idea that if you are one type of scientist, you are a big child, and no matter how convenient the idea that if you are another type of scientist, you manage to be a man, these ideas are not facts, they are metaphors.

So, it seems that Weber does not manage to limit himself to facts, even inconvenient ones. When at his most committed to helping us judge a phenomenon, even someone who claims that his method consists of observing facts, ends up relying on metaphors. Does this failure to fully appreciate his own method adversely affect his judgment? We need to consider how apt Weber's metaphors are. In arriving at the images of, on the one hand, those who are big children and, on the other hand, those who are men, Weber must have in mind the point that scientists like him are willing to face inconvenient facts, such as that Jews cannot become academics, mediocrities get promoted, politicians cannot avoid utilizing violence, and scientists cannot find the way to happiness. It can be conceded that, in facing these things, they are more like men than like big children. However, it is the case that there is a glaring passivity to these responses.[6] In all the examples, he seems resigned. In the first two cases, he seems willing to swallow clear injustices. In the third and fourth cases, he does not seem at all inclined even to try to imagine how it could be otherwise. Recalling that, in another context, Weber himself depicted 'manly conduct' as when one is willing to actively 'resist evil' (Weber 1947a: 148), we can wonder whether, even in his own terms, it is all that informative to depict his own, actually quite passive, sort of behavior as acting like a man.

The underlying problem here might stem from the differing requirements attached to understanding oneself as working with facts and understanding oneself as working with metaphors. Unlike apt metaphors, many facts do have an either/or quality. For example, if one can satisfy oneself of the fact that a male X is not a big child, one can be fairly sure that he must be a man. On the other hand, that he is not *like* a big child does not mean that the most apt metaphor for him will be that what he is like is a man. Even though it is evident to us that, in this example, Weber is not working with facts, given his avowed method, he may either not know what he is doing or, even if he does, may not be aware that what he is doing in this case requires a different mode of thinking than the one he is accustomed to. He may think that, as in factual reasoning, not being a big child is all we need to know in order to judge. He may imagine it 'proves' what he is. The upshot is that he rests content with an overly complacent image of himself.

Notes

1   My understanding of Weber's analysis owes much to Blum and McHugh (1984: 66–72).
2   As we shall see, Weber here shows a much broader understanding of what can be intelligible than we saw with Macintyre in Chapter 5.
3   Weber is quoting the slogan at the entrance to Hell in Dante's *Inferno*: Abandon all hope.
4   In the event, Justice Kennedy voted against the reforms though they got through anyway.
5   However, in the next chapter, we will argue that there is a kind of neutrality that the authors of good metaphors *do* achieve.
6   Relevant here is Blum's interpretation of this passage in which he suggests that it shows Weber is committed to 'enduring,' or, in other words that scientists should 'adapt to the circumstances without respect to their quality or value' (Blum 1977: 111).

Chapter 11

Bad Metaphors

While we have been advocating metaphoric reasoning and have mostly discussed what we consider apt metaphors, we have never denied that there can be bad metaphors. This possibility, addressed only sporadically so far, is the explicit topic of this chapter. We approach it by introducing an author who eventually became disillusioned with metaphors. George Lakoff was the co-author of a book that proposes 'that metaphor is pervasive in everyday life, and not just in language but in thought and action. Our ordinary conceptual system, in terms of which we both think and act, is fundamentally metaphorical in nature' (Lakoff and Johnson 1980: 3).

As such, these authors conclude that

> it is as though the ability to comprehend experience through metaphor were a sense, like seeing or touching or hearing, with metaphors providing the only ways to perceive and experience much of the world. Metaphor is as much a part of our functioning as our sense of touch, and as precious. (Lakoff and Johnson 1980: 239)

However, some years later Lakoff seems much more reserved in his assessment of metaphors. Instead of being precious, he now suggests that 'metaphorical thought, in itself, is neither good nor bad; it is simply commonplace and inescapable' (Lakoff, 1991a: 2).

What has led to this change of heart is his observation of the way metaphors were used in the build-up to the first Gulf War. He has come to realize that

> metaphors can kill. The discourse over whether to go to war in the Gulf has a panorama of metaphor. Secretary of State Baker saw Saddam Hussein as 'sitting on our economic lifeline.' President Bush portrayed him as having a 'stranglehold' on our economy. General Schwarzkopf characterized the occupation of Kuwait as a 'rape' that was on-going [...] Saddam Hussein was painted as a Hitler. (Lakoff 1991a: 1–2)

Lakoff's sense is that all of these metaphors hide 'realities in a harmful way' (Lakoff 1991a: 2) and he therefore, understandably, attempts to work out what is wrong with them. For example, one of his reasons for concluding that the Saddam/Hitler comparison is a bad one is that 'Iraq wasn't Germany. It has 17 million people, not 70 million' (Lakoff 1991b: 2).

While one cannot deny that he, here, manages to locate a factual difference between Iraq and Germany, since it would not even be a *metaphor* if there were no differences between

Iraq and Germany it is hard to see how merely noting a difference can indicate that there is anything wrong with the metaphor.

Bad metaphors may well 'hide realities' but it would have to be in another way than by ignoring existing factual discrepancies between the two things being compared. Whereas Lakoff and Johnson resist the idea that 'metaphor is […] a device of the poetic imagination […] a matter of extraordinary rather than ordinary language' (Lakoff and Johnson 1980: 3), we have treated metaphor as best seen as, essentially, an aesthetic device. Therefore, in order to work out how bad metaphors might hide reality, it could be necessary to understand the relationship of good metaphors and, indeed, aesthetic methods as a whole, to reality.[1]

Highly relevant here is Maurice Blanchot's idea that art provides us with *images* of reality, provided we do not interpret his idea that art gives us images of things as 'on a path leading us back to suppositions happily abandoned, analogous to the one which used to define art as imitation, a copy of the real' (Blanchot 1982: 34, footnote).

Picasso's *Guernica (1937)* certainly does not provide a copy of civil war. Yet it certainly does provide us with an image of it. It aids understanding by visualizing it, thereby helping us to imagine what it is like. And it is not just painting that can do this. So, T. S. Eliot's poem 'The Hollow Men' (1925) provides us with an image of what the ending of the world could be like, i.e. that it would end with a whimper rather than a bang. Or Carson McCullers's novel *The Heart is a Lonely Hunter (1940)* provides an image of what a particular kind of love, namely one-way love, is like. It is images like these, none of which are copies, that Blanchot sees art as providing.

As a start toward understanding how an image can be informative about an object—some reality—without copying it, Blanchot suggests:

> We might […] recall that a tool, when damaged, becomes its *image* […] In this case the tool, no longer disappearing into its use, *appears*. This appearance of the object is that of resemblance […] The category of art is linked to this possibility for objects to 'appear,' to surrender, that is, to the pure and simple resemblance behind which there is nothing—but being. (Blanchot 1982: 258–9, original emphasis)

When we have an image of a thing, then, the thing appears to us in the form of its being. Picasso, Eliot, and McCullers all manage to let their subjects appear, and when the subjects do so, we can be said to glimpse something of these subjects' being. The other important matter that is being alluded to here is that the reason we do not normally possess an image of a thing is because it is 'disappearing into its use.' Normally, things are not 'abandoned' (Blanchot 1982: 259) in this way.

If this process of not letting a thing disappear into its use is what is essential to the production of its image, there would be major consequences for what activity is required in order to manage to be an artist. Blanchot depicts this demanding and admittedly strange process, adopting as his chief spokespersons two exceptionally self-aware artists, Kafka and Rilke. According to Kafka: 'To the extent that, being a writer, he does justice to what requires writing, he can never again express himself' (Blanchot 1982: 26–7).

Whereas we are accustomed to think of art as 'subjective' as distinct from the 'objectivity' of science, Kafka says his art requires him *not* to express himself. But this form of non self-expression is clearly different from that of an 'objective' observer because it provides him with access to 'the pure passivity of being' (Blanchot 1982: 27).

We can further understand the need for this loss of self because, according to Rilke:

The work requires of the writer that he lose everything he might construe as his own 'nature,' that he lose all character and that, ceasing to be linked to others and to himself by the decision which made him an 'I,' he becomes the empty place where the impersonal affirmation emerges. (Blanchot 1982: 55)

And we can further understand that this type of loss of self—this becoming impersonal—provides a completely different sort of access to things than the neutrality of the scientific observer because reality will no longer look as it ordinarily does. When he becomes 'impersonal' or 'disinterested' or even 'insouciant' (Blanchot 1982: 175), 'the humble and outworn realities' (139) 'lose their use value, their falsified nature, and lose also their narrow boundaries in order to penetrate into their true profundity' (139).

So when the writer ceases to be self-expressive, when she becomes impersonal, objects can appear in their being much like, as we just saw with a tool when it is no longer usable, we get its image and that lets the tool appear. So, although the writer is not seeing things as they ordinarily are seen, i.e. in terms of use, 'this does not mean that everything sinks into the void. On the contrary, things then offer themselves in the inexhaustible fecundity of their meaning which our vision ordinarily misses' (Blanchot 1982: 151). If one is unwilling or unable to adopt a gaze 'ceasing to direct itself forward with the pull of time that attracts it to goals' (151), one will have no ability to have access to such images.

Aesthetic impersonality as we are coming to understand it, needs to be differentiated from some versions of impersonality that Sharon Cameron has identified. For example, the 18th-century theologian, Jonathan Edwards, advocates impersonal love. This is not typical human love—strong affection for a person—but 'love without particularity' (Cameron 2007: 23). It is hard to see how love could take this form because being directed toward particular objects seems inherent in the very idea of love. It seems vacuous and not really love at all if it is directed toward everyone and everything. Edwards tries to defend what seems impossible by urging us to base our love not on particular qualities of persons that have resonance for us but on how virtuous each person is. He formulates this as the way 'in which God himself exercises love' (33). However, as Cameron points out, that seems to require calculations that are both impossible to execute and, even if they could be executed, seem too mechanistic to amount to love (28).

Problems with his version of impersonality aside, what Edwards expects needs to be distinguished from what artists do. While, as with our example of McCullers, an artist's subject can of course be love, the aesthetic stance is not achieved just by expressing love, whether of the human or godlike variety.

There are two aspects to another thinker's, Ralph Waldo Emerson's, advocacy of impersonality. First, he denies that personal identity even exists. Using as evidence a typical person's moods that, admittedly, do vary, he denies the 'continued existence of a separately existing self' (Cameron 2007: 79). Second, he offers compensation for abandoning this supposedly illusory self. As we 'forget ourselves' (94), we attain 'access to something higher' (96) by resisting 'the usurpation of the particular' (90). But, as Cameron points out, in this 'higher' state, there is a tendency to end up 'imperiously dismissing others' interest' (101) and this can often take the form that 'what is being made light of is someone else's pain' (100).

Emerson is impersonal in the sense of being above it all. This is not where the artist places herself as witness the fact that there is no lack of sensitivity to others' suffering, for example in *Guernica* or *The Heart is a Lonely Hunter*. Furthermore, while artists are not expressing their selves, this is not to say they do not have them.

Like artists, Simone Weil does not deny the existence of the self. However, she does try to annihilate it, using a process she calls 'de-creation' (Cameron 2007: 110). The way she achieves this is by voluntary suffering. Suffering is worthwhile because it is 'the moment when the body can't escape registration of what is other than itself. Suffering is defined as what the body can't escape incorporating—the body coming into being in relation to its permeability' (132).

While one feels the pain, it is as if one's self is gone because the pain 'engrosses all feeling and every other aspect of the person' (Cameron 2007: 136). In this permeable state, one gets freed for 'some authentic presence' (137) that to Weil means being 'devoured by God' (123).

In the artist, while refraining from self expression is certainly meant to make one permeable to what is other, i.e. the identity—the being—of things, in that there is always an author, there is no complete annihilation of self nor is the artist's mode of access by suffering any more than it is by loving.

Finally, there is T. S. Eliot's version of impersonality, as displayed in his *Four Quartets (1943)* period. Here, Cameron finds 'a disarticulation of any kind of entity' (Cameron 2007: 149), i.e. of all things and not just selves. Things, including selves, 'are no sooner established than they begin to come undone' (151). As her key example, Cameron cites Eliot's portrayal of a ghost in the second *Quartet*. Though the figure presented here is meant to allude to a scene in Dante where Dante suddenly recognizes that one shade is his former teacher, in Eliot's treatment the point is that the ghost can *not* be recognized. Eliot himself calls the figure 'compound' (Eliot, 'Little Gidding', v.II). As Cameron interprets it: 'The Ghost's compositional nature prohibits his wholeness or completion—qualities all the more compromised by his self-description of being constituted through a passage, a going back and forth, in a redundancy without closure' (164).

In attempting to articulate Eliot's concept of the impersonal as displayed in his rendition of a ghost, Cameron actually references Blanchot. She writes that Eliot's ghost is 'unlike

Blanchot's "neutral" [...] for the ghost, in so far as he is anything at all, is best expressed as pure changing' (Cameron 2007: 165).

It is right that to be impersonal in Blanchot's sense is not a matter of lacking lasting substance. Thus, Blanchot remarks on the fact that, without it being right to conclude that what is continually appearing is the artist's self, an artist can still have a recognizable style, indeed can even be seen, in distinct works, to be repeating herself (Blanchot 1982: 24).

The reason Cameron comes to cite Blanchot in her discussion of Eliot is because she has found a passage where he, too, references a ghost. Besides the passage confirming Cameron's point that Blanchot's neutral cannot be characterized as pure changing, it can also help us further develop how his neutral *can* be characterized. And, as we shall see, what Blanchot is doing is doubly interesting for us because how he characterizes the impersonal here utilizes metaphors. In the build-up to the passage that Cameron cites, what is striking Blanchot is that what the lack of self—the kind of impersonal—of the aesthetic stance is *like* is the voice of the narrator in the typical novel. Blanchot's impersonal is like a narrator in that the narrator's 'relation to life would be a neutral one' (Blanchot 1993: 380), in the way this voice speaks 'the meaning of what is and what is said is still given, but from out of a withdrawal' (380).

What is withdrawn is the self or, if it is not, what results is a bad narrative:

Often in a bad narrative [...] we have the impression that someone is speaking and prompting the characters, or even the events with what they are to say: an indiscreet and awkward intrusion. We say that it is the author speaking, an authoritarian and complacent 'I' still anchored. (Blanchot 1993: 380)

On the other hand, in good narrative

the impression is that someone is talking 'in the background' [...] outside 'in back,' which is in no way a space of domination or a lofty space from which one might grasp everything in a single glance and command the events. (Blanchot 1993: 380)

His further idea, and it is here that we arrive at the passage Cameron cites, is that to adopt this narrator-like stance is rather like being a ghost because the artist's self

always tends to absent itself in its bearer and also efface him as the center; it is thus neutral in the decisive sense that it cannot be central, does not create a center, does not speak from out of a center, but, on the contrary, at the limit, would prevent the work from having one; withdrawing from it every privileged point of interest. (Blanchot 1993: 386)

A voice that manages not to create a center, and especially does not make *itself* the center, is probably Blanchot's clearest image of the kind of impersonality the aesthetic stance achieves.

This is different from Edwards because it cannot be identified with any kind of love; different from Emerson because it is more a matter of coming from the side or outside than being above it all and because it is not at all dismissive of particular human experiences; different from Weil because it is an intact voice rather than annihilated and not a product of its own suffering; different from Eliot because both it and the things it portrays have substance.

Furthermore, that, as Blanchot says, the meaning of things *is* available to the narrator suggests a very basic way in which aesthetic neutrality is different, not just from the forms of impersonality Cameron discusses, but also from the scientific ideal of objectivity. Scientific objectivity, famously, demands approaching things while being totally 'value-free.' The trouble with such a stance is that it rules out seeing the meaning (as distinct from the physical or behavioral appearance) of virtually anything. As Charles Taylor points out: 'With terms like "courage" or "brutality" or "gratitude" we cannot grasp what would hold all the instances together as a class if we prescind from their evaluative point' (Taylor 1989: 54).

This means that the '"descriptive" meaning cannot be separated from the "evaluative"' (Taylor 1989: 54). Pure scientific objectivity, even though it purports to manage to produce descriptions, would not even allow an observer to report that X is courageous, brutal, or grateful whereas there would be innumerable instances of narrators arriving at conclusions like these without it amounting to an awkward intrusion; a case of an author's self speaking.

There are also many, indeed too many, works of art, paintings, poems, novels, etc. that let us see only an artist's self, his likes, his dislikes, his opinions, some goal he has in mind. These artists are not willing or able to become what Blanchot formulates as impersonal. In such cases, though the subjects of their work may be clear, we do not feel we learn much, if anything, about what these subjects are like. Instead of illuminating anything, such work appears ponderous, heavy-handed. The artist's hand intrudes and, when this happens, nothing other than the artist's own efforts, opinions, and desires manage to appear. In Blanchot's terms, the artist has become like a bad narrator.

We suggest that *this* is the problem that is afflicting the metaphors of President Bush and his associates. Their selves are intruding rather than withdrawing. They are not at all disinterested or impersonal and, needless to say, they are certainly not insouciant in their method of gazing at Hitler and Saddam. Instead, they want to use them as tools, to appropriate them for goals of their own. Lakoff notes but does not reflect on his impression that 'as the Gulf crisis developed, President Bush tried to justify going to war' (Lakoff 1991a: 5).

To try to justify is different from trying to judge. Judgment, as we now see thanks to Blanchot, requires the type of disinterest or impersonality exemplified by artists in their approach to things. It requires refraining from using things just to further one's goals. Only by so doing can one arrive at images—appearances that are not normally visible—of things, and that access to what Blanchot (and also Heidegger)[2] depict as things' being. Accessing these images is the key step in going on to judge rather than merely justify things.

As we saw in the last chapter, Weber has identified various ways in which action can be oriented that do not depend on metaphoric reasoning. When metaphors are used merely to justify actions, it is likely that the actual motive for the action would be one of these modes of orientation, albeit with the action executed without the attention to inconvenient facts that Weber himself would wish to be there. For example, in the case of Bush, the cause could be an emotional orientation: anger at Saddam's effrontery. Alternatively, as many have speculated, he could have had some form of what Weber would consider a rational orientation, perhaps using war as a means toward the goal of protecting US oil interests or even treating war with Saddam as a means toward the goal of expunging the notion, prevalent among many at the time, that the president was a wimp.

Strong suspicions that a metaphor is being used to justify rather than judge should arise whenever the proposed comparison seems to do little to illuminate what the objects in question, e.g. Hitler, Saddam, are actually like. This would be the case because one's actual interest is not to work out (disinterestedly) the nature of phenomena, not to work to identify things by attending to differences and similarities, especially ones that are not immediately apparent, but rather to exploit a similarity, e.g. that two persons both happened to start wars, in order to provide an acceptable rationale for a course of action.[3]

However, it cannot be denied that metaphors are effective and tempting tools that can be exploited for this purpose because, even when a comparison is clearly not illuminating, resisting it will never be a matter just of pointing to factual discrepancies between the things being compared. Since, as we said, metaphors are not copies, the limit of all metaphors is such that the things being compared are never exactly alike. Metaphors used to justify will be ponderous, heavy-handed, often transparently self-serving, and so not revealing about the meaning of anything, but that is not to say one will ever be able to say they are exactly wrong.

But is it really possible to judge in the way we are proposing, i.e. by developing images of the relevant actors, in such an admittedly fraught situation as when the issue is whether or not to go to war? Can the aesthetic approach, with the form of indifference it requires, ever be adopted in such a case? Arguably, some work by a military strategist, Jeffrey Record, shows it is indeed possible. He depicts Hitler as follows:

> Hitler was simultaneously unappeasable and undeterrable—a rare combination that made war the only means of bringing him down. He understood that he could not achieve his international ambitions without war, and no territorial or political concessions the democracies might offer him would ever be enough. (Record 2008: 94)

That there could be someone who is both unappeasable and undeterrable amounts to an *image* of Hitler. It is, in other versions, a version of what Hitler is like. And if Hitler is like this, it becomes at least feasible to work out—to judge—to what extent others might be like this too. That is, we do not need to conclude (President Bush's mistake) that virtually everyone who starts a war is like this because, after all, they do have something in common with him, i.e. starting a war. Nor are we fated to conclude (Lakoff's mistake) that there is no one like this because, unavoidably, there will always be some differences between Hitler and anyone else with whom one might be inclined to compare him.

In practice, Record discovers that, not just Saddam, but also another leader to whom the Hitler analogy was applied, Ho Chi Minh, is best seen as not all that similar to him:

> Ho's ambitions were limited, and his fighting power local, whereas Saddam was never in a position to overcome US military domination of the Persian Gulf. Saddam may have been as bloody-minded as Hitler, but his power always fell short of his ambitions. If Ho was undeterrable in his quest for a reunified Vietnam under Communist auspices (a fact that escaped proponents of US military intervention), Saddam proved vulnerable to credible deterrence because he always loved himself more than he hated the United States. (Unlike Hitler, he preferred surrender and captivity to suicide.) (Record 2008: 94)

Briefly put, when we form an image of Ho, we can appreciate that he is not all that Hitler-like because, while he was probably equally undeterrable, he did not share Hitler's ambitions to conquer the world. He only wanted to unify Vietnam. When we form an image of Saddam, we can appreciate that he, too, is not all that Hitler-like because, whereas he was perhaps nearly as ambitious (at least for regional domination), he was much more vulnerable to deterrence, an example being the fact that it turns out that the threat of invasion and sanctions did cause him to destroy his weapons of mass destruction.

Credible comparisons such as these with Hitler can have practical consequences. They enable us to judge, rather than merely justify, actions. In this case, a realization that Ho, on the one hand, could not be deterred from his aim of unifying Vietnam but, on the other hand, had no wish to do anything more ambitious than that, means that it was not worth going to war with him. Similarly, a realization that Saddam, however ambitious, was susceptible to forms of deterrence much less drastic than outright war means that it was not worth going to war with him either.

Now we can better understand why Dante has pride of place in this work. It is for demonstrating that even an author who presumes to make ultimate judgments on persons' lives need not be presumptuous if he manages to base his conclusions, not on his own desires, goals, or beliefs but on a consideration, best described as aesthetic, of what those persons' lives were like.

Notes

1   It should be stressed that, while at this point we are discussing aesthetic method in general, that is certainly not to suggest that metaphors are the only aesthetic technique.
2   For example in *Being and Time* (Heidegger 1962).
3   Nussbaum's plant metaphor, discussed in Chapter 8, would be another case in point. The unilluminating metaphor is probably a result of her excessive interest in justifying her belief that we humans are tragic.

References

Alpers, Svetlana (1983) *The Art of Describing in Dutch Art in the 17th Century* Chicago: University of Chicago Press.

Arendt, Hannah (1965) *Eichmann in Jerusalem* Harmondsworth: Penguin.

—— (1978) *The Life of the Mind* London: Harcourt.

—— (1982) *Lectures on Kant's Political Philosophy* Brighton: Harvester.

Aristotle (1958) 'Poetics' in *On Poetry and Style* Trans. G. M. A. Grube, New York: Bobbs-Merrill, 3–62.

—— (1976) *Ethics* Trans. J. A. K. Thomson, Harmondsworth: Penguin.

Barthelme, Donald (1968) *Snow White* London: Cape.

Beiner, Ronald (1983) *Political Judgement* London: Methuen.

Beiner, Ronald and Nedelsky, Jennifer (2001) *Judgment, Imagination, and Politics* London: Rowman and Littlefield.

Belotti, Elena (1978) *What Are Little Girls Made Of?* New York: Schocken Books.

Benvenuto, Bice and Kennedy, Roger (1986) *The Works of Jacques Lacan* London: Free Association Books.

Bettelheim, Bruno (1991) *The Uses of Enchantment* London: Penguin.

Birchall, B. C. (1981) 'Hegel's Notion of *Aufheben*' *Inquiry* 24.1, 75–103.

Blanchot, Maurice (1982) *The Space of Literature* Lincoln: University of Nebraska Press.

—— (1993) *The Infinite Conversation* Minneapolis: University Of Minnesota Press.

Blum, Alan (1974) *Theorizing* London: Heinemann.

—— (1977) 'Criticalness and "Traditional Prejudice": Science as the Perfect Art for our Times' *Canadian Journal of Sociology* 2.1, 97–124.

—— (2011) *The Grey Zone of Health and Illness* Bristol: Intellect.

Blum, Alan and McHugh, Peter (1984) *Self-Reflection in the Arts and Sciences* New Jersey: Atlantic Highlands.

Cameron, Sharon (2007) *Impersonality: Seven Essays* London: University of Chicago Press.

Carnap, Rudolf (1959) 'The Elimination of Metaphysics Through Logical Analysis of Language' in A. J. Ayer, ed. *Logical Positivism* Glencoe: The Free Press, 60–81.

Clarendon Press (1993) *The New Shorter Oxford English Dictionary* Oxford: Clarendon Press.

Dante (1955)[c.1315] *Purgatory* Trans. Dorothy Sayers, Harmondsworth: Penguin.

—— (1962)[c.1321] *Paradise* Trans. Dorothy Sayers and Barbara Reynolds, Harmondsworth: Penguin.

—— (1979)[c.1314] *Hell* Trans. Dorothy Sayers, Harmondsworth: Penguin.

—— (1986)[c.1321] *Paradise* Trans. Mark Musa, Harmondsworth: Penguin.

De Man, Paul (1978) 'The Epistemology of Metaphor' *Critical Inquiry* 5.1, 13–30.

Derrida, Jacques (1982) *Margins of Philosophy* Brighton: Harvester Press.

—— (1991) 'Interpretations at War: Kant, the Jew, the German' *New Literary History* 22.1, 39–96.

Didi-Huberman, Georges (2005) *Confronting Images* University Park: Penn State Press.

Dworkin, Ronald (2012) 'Why the Mandate is Constitutional: The Real Argument' *New York Review of Books* LIX.8, 4–8.

Gadamer, Hans-Georg (1989) *Truth and Method* London: Sheed and Ward.

Giddens, Anthony (1991) *Modernity and Self-Identity* Cambridge: Polity.

Hegel, Georg Wilhelm Friedrich (1892)[1816] *The Logic of Hegel* Oxford: The Clarendon Press.

Heidegger, Martin (1961) *An Introduction to Metaphysics* New York: Anchor Books.

—— (1962) *Being and Time* London: Basil Blackwell.

—— (1969) *Identity and Difference* New York: Harper and Row.

Kafka, Franz (1978) *Letters to Friends, Family, and Editors* London: John Calder.

Kripke, Saul (1977) 'Identity and Necessity' in Stephen Schwartz, ed. *Naming, Necessity, and Natural Kinds* Ithaca: Cornell University Press, 66–101.

Lacan, Jacques (1977) *Ecrits: A Selection* London: Tavistock.

Lakoff, George and Johnson, Mark (1980) *Metaphors We Live By* London: University of Chicago Press.

Lakoff, George (1991a) 'Metaphor and War: The Metaphor System Used to Justify War in the Gulf' Part 1 *Viet Nam Generation Journal and Newsletter* 3.3.

—— (1991b) 'Metaphor and War: The Metaphor System Used to Justify War in the Gulf' Part 2 *Viet Nam Generation Journal and Newsletter* 3.3.

Leibniz, Gottfried (1956) [1717] *The Leibniz-Clarke Correspondence* Manchester: Manchester University Press.

Macintyre, Alasdair (1985) *After Virtue* London: Duckworth.

McHugh, Peter (2005) 'Shared being, old promises, and the just necessity of affirmative action' *Human Studies* 28.2, 129–56.

—— (2007) 'Intimacy' Unpublished Paper York University.

—— (2008) 'Furthermores on the Aesthetic' Unpublished Paper York University.

Menke, Christoph (1998) *The Sovereignty of Art* Cambridge: MIT Press.

Morris, Benny (1987) *The Birth of the Palestinian Refugee Problem 1947–9* Cambridge: Cambridge University Press.

Norval, Aletta (2010) 'A Democratic Politics of Acknowledgment: Political Judgement, Imagination, and Exemplarity' *Diacritics* 38.4, 59–76.

Nussbaum, Martha, (1986) *The Fragility of Goodness* Cambridge: Cambridge University Press.

Oz, Amos (2004) *Help Us To Divorce* London: Vintage.

Plato (1949) *Theatetus* Trans. Benjamin Jowett, Indianapolis: Bobbs-Merrill.

—— (1970) 'Philebus' in *The Dialogues of Plato, Vo. 3 Timaeus and Other Dialogues* Trans. Benjamin Jowett, London: Sphere Books, 49–118.

—— (1973) 'Laches' in *Laches and Charmides* Trans. Rosemary Sprague, New York: Bobbs-Merrill, 13–49.

—— (1976) *The Republic* Trans. Desmond Lee, Harmondsworth: Penguin.

Record, Jeffrey (2008) 'Retiring Hitler and "Appeasement" from the National Security Debate' *Parameters* 38.2, 91–101.

Ricoeur, Paul (1978) *The Rule of Metaphor* London: Routledge and Kegan Paul.

Rosen, Stanley (1969) *Nihilism* New Haven: Yale University Press.

Sandel, Michael (1996) *Democracy's Discontent* London: Harvard University Press.

Searle, John (1979) *Expression and Meaning: Studies in the Theory of Speech Acts* Cambridge: Cambridge University Press.

Sontag, Susan (1967a) *Against Interpretation and other Essays* London: Eyre and Spottiswoode.

—— (1967b) 'Partisan Review Forum on Vietnam' *Partisan Review* XXXIV.1, 51–8.

—— (1977) *Illness as Metaphor* New York: Farrar, Strauss, and Giroux.

—— (1988) *Aids and its Metaphors* London: Allen Lane.

Taylor, Charles (1989) *Sources of the Self* Cambridge: Harvard University Press.

Torrey, Norman (1946) 'Introduction' in *Candide* New York: Appleton Century Crofts, IX–X.

Voltaire (1946) [1759] *Candide* New York: Appleton Century Crofts.

Weber, Max (1947a) 'Science as a Vocation' in *From Max Weber* London: Kegan Paul, 129–58.

—— (1947b) *The Theory of Social and Economic Organization* New York: Free Press.

—— (1947c) 'Politics as a Vocation' in *From Max Weber* London: Kegan Paul, 77–128.

Williams, Charles (1943) *The Figure of Beatrice* London: Faber and Faber.

Wittgenstein, Ludwig (1958) *Philosophical Investigations* London: Macmillan.